Perfect Phrases for Building Strong Teams

Hundreds of Ready-to-Use Phrases for Fostering Collaboration, Encouraging Communication and Growing a Winning Team

Linda Eve Diamond

McGraw-Hill

New York Chicago San Francisco Lisbon
London Madrid Mexico City Milan New Delhi
San Juan Seoul Singapore Sydney Toronto

The **McGraw·Hill** *Companies*

1 2 3 4 5 6 7 8 9 0   FGR/FGR   0 9 8 7

ISBN-13: 978-0-07-149073-3
ISBN-10: 0-07-149073-6

This book is printed on acid-free paper.

McGraw-Hill books are available at special quantity discounts to use as premiums and sales promotions, or for use in corporate training programs. For more information, please write to the Director of Special Sales, Professional Publishing, McGraw-Hill, Two Penn Plaza, New York, NY 10121-2298. Or contact your local bookstore.

Library of Congress Cataloging-in-Publication Data

Diamond, Linda Eve.
    Perfect phrases for building strong teams/by Linda Eve Diamond.
        p. cm.
ISBN 0-07-149073-6 (alk. paper)
1. Teams in the workplace. 2. Interpersonal communication. I. Title.

HD66.D527 2008
658.4'022–dc22   2007001154

Contents

Contents

Part Two: Building Strong Teams   15

Chapter 3: Building Your Team   17

Chapter 4: Conflict Resolution   33

Chapter 5: Empowerment   55

Chapter 6: Feedback   67

Contents

Chapter 7: Team Process 83

Chapter 8: Virtual Team Building 99

Chapter 9: Perks, Benefits, and Rewards 115

Contents

Preface

Whether you're in the process of building a new team or strengthening your existing team, nothing is more powerful than the words and actions of a leader with a strong team mindset. The fact that you're holding this book is a testament to your interest in creating a strong team.

Strong teams are the products of strong leadership. This does not mean taking on the position of the omniscient, working 24/7, in charge of all things large and small. It means, instead, developing a team that is strong and autonomous, with the knowledge and authority to make decisions. The strong leader builds trust and confidence in the team. The strong team leader is not threatened by team member talent, but realizes that a leader's power is intensified by the work of capable team members.

The essential nature of strong teams is the same, whatever your business, whatever your industry. Do your words and mindsets inspire team behavior? Never underestimate the strength of your words. Do you inspire? Do you ask the right questions? Does your team have the freedom to be creative? Do they have the tools to achieve your desired goals? You, as team leader, must ask yourself these questions as you continue to build your team.

Who Can Use This Book?

This book is designed for small and large business owners, the self-employed who rely on others (whether routinely or on a per-project basis), executives, department managers, and anyone who takes on the role of building and enhancing a strong team. Whether you are running one team, large or small, a number of teams, an ongoing team, or intermittent teams, success depends upon your team leadership skills.

The team mindsets and phrases can be used by team leaders in any industry; and most of the targeted phrases can be easily adapted to suit your needs. Please accept the broad use of the words *clients* and *customers*. I often refer to them interchangeably.

Book Map

Part One: Who Is On Your Team?

The first section of *Perfect Phrases for Building Strong Teams* helps you clarify who is on your team. Everyone who has an interest in your team's success is connected with your team. From clients and customers to networking opportunities and advisory boards, think about who is—and could be—on your team. The next step in the team leader's mindset for building strong teams is to understand the stages of team development, which are outlined here.

Part Two: Building Strong Teams

This section, the heart of *Perfect Phrases*, begins with assembling your team and leads you through conflict resolution, building confidence and competence, establishing effective team processes and encouraging creativity. A strong team network, an inspiring leader, and the positive reinforcement encouraged in these mindsets and phrases motivates team members to give their best. Additional team motivators discussed include perks, benefits, and rewards. The virtual team building chapter is useful for teams that operate entirely or partially online and in the same vicinity or across time zones.

Part Two ends with a chapter about team rewards and includes monetary or physical rewards and recognition. Rewards and incentives motivate teams to strive. Of course, so do the other elements of team building. Your team will be motivated by inspiring team processes, a leader who listens, and the myriad of team-centered ideas in this book, as well as ideas you have on your own and will find elsewhere. However, the additional power of perks, rewards, and incentives is that they show your appreciation and give deserving team members something extra for their effort. A hard-working team deserves nothing less.

Part Three: Team-Building Exercises

Would your team benefit by bringing in a team-building professional? The book's final section offers an overview of more formal (and informal) team-building exercises. This section also offers questions and insights to help you decide and, if it's right for you, to find the best professional for your needs. Learn about different types of team-building exercises and how you can follow-up and follow-through after an exercise or series of exercises, integrating the experience into your team's everyday processes. In the spirit of turning things upside-down and looking at them differently, the book ends with icebreakers, a team process suggestion you will come across in the book.

Enter Here

Perfect Phrases for Building Strong Teams is an easy-to-carry, easily referenced resource for team builders. Whatever your business, whatever your goals, your leadership is the key to building a powerful team. Your willingness to learn and expand your expertise and knowledge of teams—picking up this and other books targeted to skill-enhancement—is a testament to your ability to lead a successful team. Use or modify the phrases in this book and consider the mindsets behind them. If you're ready to build your leadership muscles, enter here.

Acknowledgments

First, I would like to thank Harriet Diamond, who was a strong team leader at Diamond Associates, Multi-Faceted Training & Consulting. I learned so much while I was part of her team, not just from creating and customizing team building programs, but from being a part of her team. Her team was both expansive and close knit as she extended it through numerous organizations and associations, many of whom she keeps in touch with even in her retirement. My thanks to my Diamond Associates teammates over the years—both those in the office and in the field as trainers, and consultants—from whom I also learned a lot about what it meant to work as a team.

Specifically, I would also like to thank some of the great teammates with whom I've been fortunate to work: Phyllis Dutwin, Nancy Barr, Marsha Fahey, Natalie Gast, and Harriet Diamond, again, as my partner on *Perfect Phrases for Motivating and Rewarding Employees*. Each of these teammates helped me grow and worked with strong team synergy.

Another team I currently work with is the International Listening Association, where the effect of listening is dynamically clear in team processes and in the overall bonding and warmth among team members.

Acknowledgments

Last, and certainly not least, I want to thank my *Perfect* editor, Donya Dickerson, who is supportive and always knows just what is needed and my agent, Grace Freedson, with deep gratitude for putting me on the *Perfect Phrases* team.

Part One

Who Is On Your Team?

Who is on your team? Let's look at your team. You have the people classified as your "work team," whether employees or a team assembled for a particular project. Think of them as your core team, but realizing that your team is more expansive than that gives you access to greater resources and more avenues for support and enthusiasm. Who else is on your team? How can you make your customers feel invested in your success? You, as the team leader, determine the scope, energy, and enthusiasm of your team.

Chapter 1

The Team Leader

"A chief is a man who assumes responsibility. He says, 'I was beaten.' He does not say, 'My men were beaten.'"
—Antoine de Saint-Exupéry

Team Leader Attitudes

Your attitude toward and understanding of team processes make the difference between a team that "goes through the motions" and one that thrives. Do you respect your team? Are you invested in team members' growth? Are you available and inspiring? Are you accountable when problems arise? A great team leader takes responsibility and shares credit.

As a leader, you set the tone for your team. What attitudes do you project? Do you use positive, encouraging words?

A leader of strong teams

- Wants to help team members achieve success
- Creates team cohesion
- Cares about the well-being of team members
- Creates a positive, inspiring atmosphere
- Respects every member of the team
- Shares credit and shoulders responsibility
- Gives team members necessary skills, then steps back to let them thrive

Strong team leaders align themselves with their teams. They consider themselves part of the team, not leaders walking out ahead. They encourage and take pride in the success of the team and its individual members. Team member success reflects well on the team, and people can sense a genuine interest in their success and well-being. Such an interest on the part of the team leader is a strong motivator.

Create a positive atmosphere for the day, the project, the vision, the goals, and the overall outlook. This would involve both something as small as the friendly "Good morning!" and as powerful as setting an expectation for whether your team's biggest challenges can be solved.

As team leader, you need to communicate with clarity and conciseness, speaking less and listening more. Great team leaders don't need to have all the answers; they just need to ask the right questions. Your role in support of the team will diminish as members gain confidence and hone team skills. Use your creative energies to assemble the best possible team and to give everyone the methods to shine as a team.

Healthy Team Development

The team goes through stages, most commonly referred to as *Forming, Storming, Norming, Performing*, and *Adjourning*. These stages were coined by Bruce Tuckman in 1965 and are still the most commonly used illustration of team development. Following is a brief overview of the stages, which you may or may not share with your team. Whether or not you do, it is helpful for you to understand the stages of team development.

Who Is On Your Team?

- *Forming* is the first stage; the forming of your team, goals, guidelines, and initial statements of expectations and establishment of roles. Team members are still acting independently in the beginning. Leadership must be strong and involved at this stage.
- *Storming* is the stage in which team members are adjusting to each other and determining roles within the team. There may be tension, power struggles, or shifting roles; this is all part of the Storming process. The team leader still needs to be the final word on decisions until a decision-making process is established and working. Some teams never leave this stage, but a strong leader can work the team through this difficult time.
- *Norming* is the stage at which things begin to settle down, and team members are functioning in their roles. At this time, adjustments can still be made, but team members know what is expected of them and how the team, as a whole, functions. Beware of the team working so hard to make things run smoothly that they enter a phase of group-think decision making. Disagreements and debates are a healthy part of team processes. As the team leader, you can often step back and allow the team to function by its own methods.
- *Performing* is the team working at optimal levels. Many of the kinks have been worked out, and this team now functions well as a unit. Communication and problem-solving channels are clear, and everyone is working together to contribute to overall team goals. You are still participating, but entrusting the team with more responsibility for its own success.

■ *Adjourning* is when a team disbands or changes at a project's completion. This is a stage worth noting. Team members feel appreciated when there is a chance to celebrate accomplishment and, if necessary, say goodbye. When focusing on or bringing closure to a project, always remember the human element. Part of adjourning on one project may involve transforming to a new one. If this stage does not apply to your team, it is especially important to celebrate even small accomplishments throughout the process.

One important point to note about these five stages is that they may not progress steadily in one direction without ever falling back. Change in leadership or any unanticipated change can throw the team back into storming or even re-forming. But a strong team won't regress for long and will progress to performing again with a little guidance, patience, and trust in the process.

Overall, keep in mind that this is a process, prone to flux and change by the simple nature of being comprised of people, most often of varied ages and backgrounds. Even those who are similar on most fronts easily vary in style. Add to the mix egos, individual goals, personality types, and personal agendas. Think of teams as living, changing organisms. You are invested in nurturing this delicate creature and drawing upon individual strengths to build a team of people acting in concert toward a particular vision or goal. Healthy team development is no small feat; it is a job for a skilled, motivated team leader.

A Model of Loyalty and Respect

Your mother was right. Treat people the way you would want to be treated. Forget power plays; you may force some modicum of false respect, but you will not gain the enthusiasm and loyalty that come from being respected and appreciated. Be a model of loyalty and respect that your team members will want to emulate. Take it beyond your immediate team by not disrespecting *anyone* in your team's presence.

You can discuss a problem with a particular client, confront a sensitive issue with a team member, or dissect with your team a situation where everything went wrong, all without showing disrespect. Be a problem solver, but don't complain, demean, or put anyone down. Earn respect by showing respect. You will also be demonstrating, for team members, delicate ways of handling sensitive issues.

Never reprimand in front of the team. Any team member problems, disciplinary actions, or developmental feedback should be handled privately. If you need to discuss the problem with your team, do so as discretely as possible.

Showing respect for your team benefits you by having team members who are motivated and respectful of you, in return. An additional benefit is that if you show respect for your team, others will, too, and that reflects on you. However, if you look at showing respect from that perspective, alone, you will come across as false and patronizing. The answer? Simple—respect your team. Every team member brings something to the table or that person wouldn't be there.

Chapter 2

Teams: The Bigger Picture

"None of us is as smart as all of us."

—Ken Blanchard

Think big. Even if expansion is not your goal, think of expanding your notions of team. This inclusive attitude may create a shift in many of your working relationships—you may be working with people you don't consider your team, informally asking for advice, or soliciting customer feedback, or asking "outsiders" for help. A small conceptual shift on your part changes your language and how integral to your success you make people feel. Strong teams are supported by a solid network.

The Extended Team

Who is working with your team? Do you have clear communication channels? Does your team know who should have easy access to information? Brainstorm a list of everyone who is or could be connected with your efforts. Reach out, when appropriate, to learn their schedules and inform them of yours. If possible, hold periodic meetings to coordinate schedules.

Do you belong to organizations that extend your reach or offer additional opportunities? Consider joining an organization that supports your interests and will offer you networking possibilities. You can join, yourself, or you can ask that team members join to make contacts and network for you. Entrusting a team member to represent you both allows you to double your efforts and shows that team member that you have the utmost confidence in him or her. One way to include your whole team is to offer a rotating schedule for team members to represent your team or attend events.

Networking groups can help connect you with other teams or with the right individuals to assist your team. A variety of networking groups are available to you. Some offer exclusive rights, where your team will be the only one from your industry, giving you the best opportunity to be the team this group will contact when in need of your expertise. Others are exclusively from your industry to offer support, a sharing of ideas, and opportunities for collaborative efforts.

The Expanded Team

A team leader is inclusive. Remember to keep broadening your definition of a team. Everyone who works toward a common goal is part of a team. You may have departments and particular work groups, so there are many layers to a team. Think of your team as rippling out in concentric circles. For example, a sales team in a tech company stretches far beyond a team of salespeople (though they do, themselves, compose one team). The team extends to include everyone who contributes to or has an interest in the final product or bottom line: product developers, the marketing department, customer service, tech support, investors, customers, administrators, personnel, suppliers, even the cleaning staff (who create a clean working environment and rely on the money coming in from product sales).

Whom can you ask for advice beyond your immediate team? Consider assembling an advisory board made up of people from any useful background. The purpose of your advisory board determines how much of your company information is accessible to the board. If you are seeking financial advice, for instance, only full disclosure to board members will enable a worthwhile endeavor.

Advisory board meetings can be called at critical stages or set at regular intervals, such as monthly. They also may take place in person, by phone, or online (either in a forum where all members are online together or where they can submit ideas any time). Find a process that suits your board and your purposes. An ongoing online discussion board would reduce the need for formal meetings, but first set reasonable expectations for how often board members check in. Offer something to advisory board members in return for their efforts, even if it is only recognition and thanks. Give them credit for their efforts for and connection to your company.

Who else is on your team? Who else is affected by your success? Is there anyone else from whom you can ask advice? Also consider hiring professionals, even on a limited basis, to have an understanding of and a hand in your team. You should have contact with a lawyer, an accountant, and a representative at your bank. Have someone you can call in case of an unexpected event or emergency.

Consumer Input

You might have an informal advisory board of consumers who offer feedback through an online forum. Bring your customers or potential customers onboard by asking their feedback. Getting client and consumer feedback has never been easier, especially with the Internet.

The tried and true methods for obtaining feedback are still in use, from paper forms to phone surveys. But consider high-tech options that may be more inviting and far-reaching, depending on who is part of your customer base. The Internet hosts a multitude of options: open your blog to comments, post a message board, e-mail customer surveys or post one on your Web site. You might want to offer a small incentive for filling out surveys. Above all, make clear that you read all messages and surveys and take consumer feedback and suggestions seriously. Some teams get their most innovative ideas (or at least the seeds for them) from customer input or requests.

What do people need? What do they want? What works? Doesn't work? Inspires customer loyalty? Turns customers off? Who knows better than your customers?

At the Center: Your Internal Team

Your internal team is the heart and soul of your operation. Never underestimate the brain power of your team. Whether or not you have a trusted advisory board, your team is still the center of your operation. A question posed to an advisory board can just as easily be posed to your team. If you have not yet given team members opportunities to shine, you may be surprised by just how strong your team's natural skills are. As you continue to strengthen your team, using the perfect phrases and mindsets, their problem-solving and idea-generating powers will continue to improve.

While this book focuses on your internal team or teams, keep in mind that your team is larger than that, and always be aware of places you or your team might reach out. Involve your internal team in this mindset. External team players are not your secret weapon; they are resources that can be cultivated and worked with by your team as well.

Part Two

Building Strong Teams

Strong leaders empower their teams to be familiar with a variety of team processes and to operate smoothly as a team. They impart those skills to team members, guiding them to success and transfer those abilities, when appropriate, to cross-cultural and virtual environments. They also provide perks, benefits, and rewards that motivate teams to excel.

You have the talent to build a strong team. The mindsets and phrases that follow will not only serve as easy reference but will also help you solidify the team mindset and hone the skill of turning the perfect phrase for building strong teams.

Chapter 3

Building Your Team

"Teamwork is no accident. It is the by-product of good leadership."

—John Adair

Though you might have the talent to take almost any group of people and turn them into a team, guaranteeing a positive outcome requires choosing the right people and training them.

If your team is already assembled, you can start from any point and turn a group of individuals into a team. If, however, you are starting from scratch, find the team members who have not only the skills to achieve team goals but also the capacity and attitude to operate as part of a team. Beyond experience, consider the ability to learn, trustworthiness, and conflict resolution skills.

Finding the right people is essential; be familiar with the concepts and question types that follow in this section so that, even if your team is assembled, you are ready if you need to hire or recruit an additional team member. As you continue to build your team, be clear about what you are looking for. If you don't know what you're looking for, how will you find it?

Once you find the right person, you, as team leader, are responsible for nurturing team members and helping them to develop talents, skills, and abilities and teaching the team methods for establishing procedures and channels.

The Team Mindset

- Ask more open than closed questions. Open questions lead to detailed answers rather than simple *yes* or *no* replies.
- Hypothetical questions are useful and can yield interesting answers, but keep in mind that you are more likely to get a response based on what the candidate thinks you want to hear than you are to find answers that reflect actual past or future performance.
- Behavioral questions (e.g., "What did you do"—*or* "How did you respond—when…") demonstrate past behavior as an indicator of future performance.
- Identify skills.
- Discuss adaptability to change.
- Find indicators of how well the prospective team member handles pressure.
- Ask team-centered questions.
- Listen more than you speak.
- Give the prospective team member an opportunity to ask questions at the end.
- Pay attention to the quality and tone of the candidate's questions.

Phrases

- "What was the most important thing you learned from your last team experience?"
- "What characteristics do you possess that you feel would be an asset to this team?"

- "What skills do you bring?"
- "On your last team, how did you see your role?"
- "What accomplishments are you most proud of in your career?"
- "Do you consider yourself a team player? Why?"
- "What complaints did you have about how your last team functioned?"
- "What leadership attributes do you possess?"
- "If a team member were in a crunch and asked you to help but your own schedule was tight, what would you do?"
- "If your team leader asked you to run a meeting, what steps would you take to ensure that everyone's ideas were heard?"
- "Were you ever in a situation that you felt under-qualified to handle? What did you do?"
- "Have you ever felt that a team member was behaving detrimentally to the team? What, if anything, did you say or do?"
- "Have you ever acted as a team leader? What can you tell me about that experience?"
- "Are you comfortable working with a team leader or team members who work from home or other remote locations?"
- "What do you know about our team?"
- "What questions do you have for me?"

The Positive Mindset

The Team Mindset

- Negativity weighs heavily and makes it hard for people to move; accomplishment becomes unnecessarily harder.
- One negative team member can hurt the whole operation.
- Some negative people can be affected by a positive atmosphere.
- Some people will always find a negative spin. Negative attitudes develop for personal reasons and often take hard work on a personal level to overcome. Inspire and be positive, but keep your expectations reasonable.
- Maintain your positive posture, even in difficult times.
- Smile.
- Use positive language.
- Be cognizant of giving positive reinforcement and praise. When things are going smoothly, it's easy to take a team's good work for granted. People want their hard work to be recognized even if—*especially* if—it looks easy.
- Praise team members for their positive outlooks; encourage positive behavior.
- In difficult situations, you don't have to smile or cover up; be honest, but maintain the team's ability to look forward and find solutions.

Phrases

- "We have no problems, only challenges."
- "Let's problem-solve together."
- "I know the timing is tight, but we can do it."

➡

- "This has been a stressful time, but today is a new day. Let's make it a good one."
- "This is a great team and I know we can meet any challenge."
- "I understand you have reservations. Let's discuss them."
- "The team has decided to move forward with this plan, so I need everyone to be positive and work to make it happen."
- "I have faith in this team."
- "If anyone has concerns, let's talk about them, problem-solve, and move forward."
- "Don't let anyone's negativity get you down. You're doing a good job under very difficult circumstances."
- "We've had a tough quarter, but with the positive changes we've been making, we should be on track within the next few months."
- "This has been a terrific week. Thanks everyone!"
- "We made the deadline just under the wire, but we made it! Fantastic work, everyone. Thank you!"
- "We've got a busy day ahead of us, but it's going to be a good one!"
- "What a hectic week! But you should all have a great sense of accomplishment. Nice work!"
- "I can see how much thought went into this design!"
- "You make this project look effortless, but I know how much work goes into it. You're doing a wonderful job!"
- "I know how difficult this [conference, database, training session, event, etc.] was to put together, even though you made it look easy. Little things always go wrong along the way, but our clients never would have known it. I'm very impressed!"

Skill Development

The Team Mindset

- Provide support or training for a team member who wants to learn.

- When you invest time, money, or other resources in people, the return on your investment comes through employees who demonstrate greater skills, knowledge, and confidence. You also show your commitment to them as valued members of the team, which will inspire their ongoing commitment to your team.

- Offering training beyond a team member's immediate position can provide insights and perspective that will help that team member contribute more fully, with a greater understanding of the process. Familiarity with the needs, processes, and expectations of other departments will help a team member work more smoothly with that department.

- Cross-training also helps team members understand customer needs and expectations. The advertising and customer service departments, for example, should know exactly what the sales team is encouraged to promise.

- Having team members ready to advance is usually an advantage over bringing in someone new.

- Some people may be more adept at one type of skill than another. When a skill is optional or easily handled by someone else, don't create feelings of inadequacy in a great team member because that skill is too challenging or beyond his or her comfort level.

- Do what you can to offer full or partial tuition reimbursement.

- Offer full or partial reimbursement for seminars and conferences.
- Encourage education.
- Bring in experts to teach the team critical skills.
- Often team members gain enough skill to function in the job, but don't have time or resources to deepen those skills. Providing the time and resources for training will benefit the team.

Phrases

- "What additional training would be beneficial to you?"
- "The upcoming training options are a great opportunity for you to position yourself to move forward."
- "Would you be interested in taking courses in our upward mobility program?"
- "I have hired a computer expert to train the team so we get the maximum benefits from our new software."
- "Would you be interested in getting your degree? We are now offering tuition reimbursement."
- "We want to invest in your talents. Would you be interested in taking courses?"
- "Since you understand the system so well, would you be willing to train other team members?"
- "To give everyone a full view of the operation and to show all avenues available to you within the company, we are offering an in-depth overview of each department at the upcoming conference."
- "Please attend some of the 'soft skill' seminars at the conference. Communication is as essential as our more technical skills."

- "You're very proficient on the computer and you certainly have all the skills to do the job. The software, though, does have much broader capabilities and I would like to send you to a class to learn more."
- "I'm sending half of the team for training. When they return, I'd like everyone with training to partner with a team member who did not have the training to teach what you have learned."
- "If you take the additional training, you will be eligible for a promotion."
- "Everyone who participates in the new training initiative will receive a special bonus."
- "I admire the extra work you put in studying on your own. I'm going to bring in a consultant to work with you on any questions you have or additional skills you'd like to learn."
- "I have built time into everyone's schedule to take the online tutorials."
- "Additional online training is available to everyone. I will have access to your progress and scores. Everyone must be completed with the first module before annual reviews."

The Learning Curve

The Team Mindset

- Every new skill takes time to learn.
- Be patient with team member learning curves.
- People learn at their own paces.
- Someone who acquires information quickly may seem ahead of someone who takes things in more slowly, but hold off judgment to see retention and application of skills.
- Don't push for speed at the cost of retention.
- People have different learning styles. Some learn best by reading on the computer, some by reading offline, and auditory learners may learn best by being told or listening to tapes.
- Repetition and hands-on learning are more effective than simple one-time instruction.
- No one should feel judged for asking questions.
- Always encourage and leave time for practice.
- Acknowledge success and accomplishment.

Phrases

- "Please ask questions."
- "Mistakes are part of learning."
- "Take adequate time to practice."
- "No one was born knowing this. We all had to learn."
- "This is not an easy skill to learn. You're all doing very well."
- "I see that you are behind in your online coursework. Do you have questions? How can I help you?"
- "I can see that you're completing your coursework far ahead of schedule. It's very impressive! But are you sure

➡

you're leaving enough time to practice and absorb each skill? You won't lose any ground if you decide to go back for additional practice."

- "I want you to feel free to ask each other questions and learn from each other."
- "There is no shame in being behind in one area. Everyone excels in certain areas and finds others more challenging."
- "I need this to be learned within a two-month time frame. If you need more time, let me know so we can arrange to get you the study time you need."
- "What questions do you have?"
- "What additional information do you need?"
- "If you need additional training, please take advantage of the group learning seminars."
- "We all learn at different paces. As long as you're meeting necessary deadlines, your pace is fine."
- "This is self-paced learning. Please do not compare your progress. Everyone has different learning styles, and some prefer more practice time than others."

Establishing Guidelines

The Team Mindset

- Have teams set or participate in setting their own guidelines.
- Determine clear guidelines for meetings to keep them on track and ensure that everyone is (and feels) treated fairly.
- Clear guidelines prevent team members from inadvertently crossing lines that were not clearly drawn.
- Let people know what is or is not acceptable and what steps will be taken if guidelines are not followed.
- Make certain the rules apply equally for everyone.
- Don't make arbitrary rules; when rules might be perceived as being arbitrary, back them up with reasons.
- Post meeting guidelines.
- New team members must be apprised verbally and in writing of the most important guidelines.
- Team members should receive complete, written guidelines.

Phrases

- "Let's establish team guidelines so that team members know what to expect and what is expected of them."
- "What problems have we encountered that would be solved by clearer guidelines?"
- "What guidelines can we establish that will make meetings run more smoothly?"
- "What guidelines can we establish that will strengthen team communication?"
- "We have run into some difficulties with doubled efforts. What guidelines can we put into place to solve that issue?"

- "Let's create some meeting guidelines that will minimize interruptions and give everyone a chance to speak."
- "These guidelines are in place to help the team function optimally, not to punish anyone."
- "What unspoken guidelines do you feel we are already following that work well?"
- "Let's break into groups and think of as many viable guidelines we can that will be helpful to the group. Then we'll pare down the list to those that are most essential."
- "Creating too many guidelines will cause the more important ones to be lost and easily forgotten."
- "A few solid, essential guidelines are worth more than a few pages of unnecessary ones."
- "We need all guidelines documented to be ready for new team members."
- "Have you had time to learn the new guidelines? Do you have any questions?"
- "Do you have any questions regarding the guidelines?"
- "We have undergone many changes since we wrote the guidelines. Please review them to see if some areas need revision."

Establishing Proper Channels

The Team Mindset

- Impose proper channels for dealing with certain problems or have the team develop channels on their own.
- New people coming into the team need to be informed of what channels have been established.
- To be fair, if you have established proper channels (for vacation requests, for example) make sure that everyone follows those channels.
- Be flexible in considering special requests and the reasons for them, but always be fair.
- If a team member hits a dead end when using proper channels, step in to help or to deal directly with the issue.
- If "proper channels" will take too long for a given situation, expedite the process.
- Be sure that proper channels are fair and unbiased.
- Sexual harassment channels must involve timely, thorough investigation and action.
- All responses to discrimination and harassment charges must be swift and fair.
- Be versed in sexual harassment and discrimination law. Even if you have others handling such complaints, learn as much as you can and be aware of what is or is not acceptable.

Phrases

- "Please go through the channels established by the team. If you hit a dead end or you have a time-sensitive

➡

issue, feel free to come to me. Otherwise, I want to respect the process established by the team."

- "If you followed proper channels and hit a dead end, I'm glad you came to me."
- "If you feel stuck in the system, come to me. No one here should ever feel caught in a maze."
- "If proper channels aren't working, we need to revise those channels."
- "I understand that you don't feel your sexual harassment report was handled fairly. I take that very seriously and will look into it immediately."
- "Thank you for bringing this to my attention. Normally this issue is reported directly to human resources, but let me help you bring this forward to them."
- "I understand the complexity of your claim. I think we should bring someone from the legal team into this discussion."
- "I wish I could help you, but this is not my department. Here is the number you need to call. If you have any problems at all going forward, please let me know and I will help move things along."
- "I wish I could honor your request, but this last-minute vacation time request will affect everyone's schedule and workload at this point. I wish you had put in the form with the necessary lead time."
- "You're right over the wire with this request, but I realize your plans came up at the last minute. Let me see what I can do."
- "That's a very serious charge and it needs to be documented and investigated. Please follow proper channels so that will happen."

➥

- "All schedule changes must be made in team meetings. You will have to wait until Wednesday's meeting unless you can get the whole team together beforehand."
- "Territories have already been assigned and we do not reassign midyear; the process is too cumbersome. You can change territories if you can find someone who wants to switch."
- "Telling me is not enough; we need the proper forms. It's better for recordkeeping and informing all concerned parties, and it saves you from relying on my memory!"
- "All team members are responsible for following up on their own requests. Nothing is official until you receive a confirmation."

Chapter 4

Conflict Resolution

"The way a team plays as a whole determines its success. You may have the greatest bunch of individual stars in the world, but if they don't play together, the club won't be worth a dime."

—Babe Ruth

Conflict is an inevitable fact of continual interaction. No two people, let alone a larger work team, can work together and avoid ever having a disagreement. The point of conflict can be a miscommunication, an error, or a clashing of ideas or desires (I want/believe/need this and you want/believe/need that). Conflict resolution involves finding the middle ground, calming heated situations, and clearing up misunderstandings. A strong team leader knows how to listen and mediate for positive solutions.

Some conflict can be caused by the technologies that are meant to help us communicate more smoothly. For instance, cell phones and e-mails, while keeping us more in touch, bring their own communication challenges: the cell phone cuts out and one person doesn't know it; the e-mail didn't get through; the tone of the e-mail is misread; the voice mail sounds hostile because of the speaker shouting through a bad connection. When working through conflict about technical difficulties, always keep in mind that misunderstandings and tensions over technical failures can begin ongoing conflicts, but proper mediation will keep resentments from building.

Establish guidelines that deter conflict over personality clashes, blame games, and competitiveness. When problems arise, proper mediation should be timely to keep team processes in check and resentments from escalating. Even more importantly, prejudices and biases should be clearly defined and deterred. No one on your team should be subjected to unfair treatment based on gender, race, or age.

Technical Difficulties

The Team Mindset

- Technical difficulties can cause us to miss important deadlines, but don't despair—call upon your team. Often, a creative solution will come from someone on the team.

- There may be a time to ask for outside help. Don't hesitate when time and reputation are on the line.

- Use solution finding as a team exercise.

- Keep your team as well equipped as possible.

- If you are continually dealing with emergencies, quick fixes, and work-arounds, consider the costs in time, team energy, and reputation. Measure those costs against the expenses of updating.

- Don't promise new equipment unless you plan to deliver.

- If technical difficulties are rooted in compatibility issues, call in an expert. Odds are that this problem will arise again. Be equipped and ready to avoid having the problem resurface.

- Don't allow one department to make promises that another cannot fulfill. Make certain that cross-departments understand each other's capabilities and that, when uncertain, team members are trained to find answers, not guess.

- A well-equipped team has confidence. They put their energies toward team goals without daily concerns about whether their equipment will support them.

- Technical difficulties are an inevitable part of business life. Plan for them. Build in time for the glitch, the breakdown, and the error message that makes no sense.

- Ensure that someone on the team is responsible for checking supplies (even with support staff, someone on the team should double-check). Never underestimate the value of having the little things in stock—like printer ink, chargers, and power cords.

Phrases

- "We know this breakdown could cause us to lose critical time. Who has a creative solution?"
- "Erin says she e-mailed and Paulo says he never received the e-mail. Let's just focus now on how to help Paulo meet his deadline." (Follow-up question: "What can we do to avoid these problems in the future?")
- "We need to upgrade our equipment. What are your recommendations—and why?"
- "Who can take on the responsibility of checking supplies? We have great equipment. Let's not be stopped by a missing wire!"
- "Does the team have the equipment it needs to function optimally?"
- "I realize the stress level is getting high because equipment seems to be working against us, but that's even more reason we need to work together!"
- "We all know that technology isn't perfect and we cannot all guarantee when we will be online, so when a message is urgent, don't just e-mail or leave a voice mail—do both."
- "If you are not getting a reply to your e-mail, try another avenue of communication."
- "We've got a breakdown and a tight timeline. There *is* a solution here. Let's take ten minutes and a deep breath, and then toss out some ideas."

- "Too much time is wasted with compatibility issues. I'm calling in an expert to help us run more smoothly."
- "I'm upgrading our systems."
- "I realize some of you hesitate to change over to our new software, but we will operate more smoothly if we're all working together in this. What does everyone need from me to facilitate a full changeover by next month?"
- "What do you think of the new Blackberries? We brought them in to streamline operations, but so far they're only complicating the issue. We can still exchange or make another support call. What are your thoughts?"
- "What is / is not working with our current technology?" "Technology is supposed to assist communication; if it gets in the way, use another method. The *purpose* is communication."

Personality Clashes

The Team Mindset

- Personality clashes, at some point, are inevitable.
- Clashes stem from any work styles, habits, speaking styles, types of humor, beliefs, or habits that differ among teammates.
- Different personalities can spur new directions, but ongoing conflict is counterproductive.
- Consultants who can work with personality clashes are well worth the investment.
- Some personality clashes can exist as a mild undercurrent without damaging the team.
- More often than not, interpersonal issues hurt the team and most can be resolved.
- Serious issues and rivalries require professional intervention.
- Make every effort to have team members resolve interpersonal issues before they poison the team.
- People rarely change, but communication styles are habits that can be practiced and developed.
- A team member who is ahead of the curve in an essential area can be an asset and an inspiration, *if* he or she is able to share knowledge without demeaning others.

Phrases

- "Different styles bring new perspectives."
- "Everyone here is an important part of this team and deserves our respect."

➥

- "I realize you have different styles. Instead of getting frustrated and trying to change each other, try to see the combination of styles as an asset."

- "I know your styles seem to clash: Ben, you work quickly and, Tracy, you're more methodical. If you can respect each other's styles and concede a little here and there, Ben will have the benefit of being slowed down to reduce errors made in haste and Tracy will have the advantage of being more aware of pace."

- "An issue with a team member's style or personality is a good opportunity to refine communication skills under difficult conditions. Some clients are bound to rub you the wrong way, too."

- "Let's focus on what needs to be done, not personalities."

- "I realize you two have issues between you, but what can you tell me that you admire or appreciate about each other?"

- "Clearly, we have a problem between you. Rhea, what would you ask Vince to do that would improve your working relationship? Vince, what would you ask of Rhea?"

- "What is at the heart of this issue? How can we resolve it?"

- "You're both great people and strong team members. This conflict is getting in your way. It interferes with the team and will hold you both back."

- "I am bringing in a consultant to work with the team's interpersonal issues."

- "Please be open and honest with our team consultant. We are not here to impress him and he can only help if we are open about the issues."

- "You are always ahead of the curve, but your team members feel like you can be condescending at times. It would benefit team morale *and* goals if you could share knowledge and expertise in a supportive manner."
- "I realize we have some long-standing resentments among team members. It's time to resolve them and move forward."
- "This team's greatest challenge is synergy. You're all problem solvers. How would you tackle this issue?"

Blame Games

The Team Mindset

- Blame games have no winners.

- While finding the source of a problem or error is usually an essential step in making the correction and ensuring future success, blaming is never helpful.

- Encourage your team members to assist one another.

- Many team members come from competitive backgrounds of winners and losers, with a sense that a mark against a teammate will add to their own stock. Discourage these notions in favor of teamwork attitudes.

- Never reprimand anyone publicly.

- Don't encourage team members who play the blame game. Don't allow team members to chastise one another.

- Beware of team members who are quick to blame others or continually single out other team members. It may be a rivalry that is unhealthy for the team.

- People make mistakes. Acknowledge that it's okay. Otherwise you will create a climate of denial and blame where everyone is so afraid to be wrong that no one is learning from mistakes.

- Some people cannot accept responsibility. Fear of being "wrong" touches on issues deeper than you will want to discuss. Work with people to create a climate where being wrong is okay and taking responsibility is rewarded, but don't push too hard when someone simply cannot admit it for fear of losing face.

- Admit your own mistakes.

Phrases

- "Let's not worry about who is at fault; let's concentrate our efforts on resolving the issue."
- "This was an error. We are all doing our best here."
- "Mistakes are an inevitable part of life and business."
- "What is important is creating fail-safes so that these errors will have less impact."
- "Please don't be afraid to ask questions; that will help us avoid mistakes."
- "Sharing information and knowledge is crucial."
- "Let's learn from each other's mistakes so that we can all be stronger as a team and as individual assets to the team."
- "I take full responsibility for this problem. It is my job to be accessible to the team when these issues arise. Let's rework our team structure so that we have clearer, tighter communication."
- "There is a big difference between responsibility and fault. Taking responsibility shows individual strength; an individual being held 'at fault' shows team weakness."
- "I want to thank Evan for catching the error so that we could rectify the problem before introducing the new product to customers."
- "Thank you all for putting in the extra effort to resolve this issue. Great work!"

Competition in the Ranks

The Team Mindset

- Looking the other way when team members steal clients or customers will build resentments and ultimately hurt the team.

- Friendly competitions to raise the bar are fine, but encouraging cutthroat behavior among team members will cause you to defeat your own purpose.

- A team that does not have zero tolerance for sabotage and discouragement will implode.

- When one team member is racing to beat another, both team members involved could end up making unnecessary errors.

- A team member who puts another down for not knowing something hurts the team.

- Team members who know more than others in an essential area should bring the others up to speed, for the good of the team.

- If someone is hoarding information to appear more indispensable than others, step in with a reminder about teamwork and team goals.

- If you run a competition among your team members, ensure that no one competes in a cutthroat fashion.

- Establishing a competition with another team will strengthen the sense of team.

- Commend collaborative efforts.

- Contests within the team should give everyone an equal chance.

- Talk about "winners" but never "losers."

- Establish rewards for everyone who exceeds a certain goal; don't limit rewards to just one top person.
- If a team member claims he or she was treated unfairly by another team member, ignoring the situation will damage trust and team spirit.
- Establish protocols of fair play.
- Work to find resolutions; if you cannot grant a resolution requested by a team member, explain why.

Phrases

- "We are here to work together, not against each other."
- "Please share your knowledge with the team."
- "We have a strong team and now we can show our strength [on the baseball field, at the bowling ally, in the competition, etc.]."
- "Because you worked together, I'm going to reward you both."
- "Though this is a competition, I still need you to support each other. We're still a team."
- "I understand you feel that Nadia stole your client. I want to hear both sides of the story."
- "Nadia, we have certain protocols of fair play. We need to find a fair resolution."
- "We have to be careful when considering whether we can reassign a client. We may have to find another alternative on this end. We cannot compromise smooth customer service or alert clients to our internal issues."
- "Let's establish, as a team, a formal Fair Play Protocol."
- "Sometimes the line is crossed unintentionally. Give your team members the benefit of the doubt."

- "I'd like to break tradition and offer you a collaborative client assignment."
- "I'm glad to see you chose to work together on this."
- "While I appreciate your extensive background, you cannot compare yourself to another team member, especially in front of a client."
- "Everyone on this team has valuable background and input."
- "Strong teams have strong support systems."

Gender Bias

The Team Mindset

- Promote a climate of equality.
- Allow for team member tasks to cross the boundaries typically assigned to men or women.
- Have a strict sexual harassment policy and clear channels for reporting.
- Make it known: gender jokes are not appropriate in the office. No one knows what might offend someone else; often the line between appropriate and inappropriate is too fuzzy for most people to recognize before they cross it.
- Be alert to gender bias: many women still face it in the form of glass ceilings and wage gaps, earning an average of 76 cents for each dollar earned by a man doing the same job.
- Women should not be referred to as "girls."
- Do not subject men to reverse discrimination in an effort to be fair to women.
- Both men and women are prone to have certain biases and stereotypes about the opposite sex. Model and promote an unbiased attitude.
- Advise people of what is acceptable and of certain words or phrasing that make others uncomfortable. For example, some men have a life-long habit of calling women "honey" or "dear." A southern man working in an office in the north may be surprised by a negative reaction to his use of these name replacements.
- Encourage patience with those making changes.

➡

Phrases

- "Everyone on this team deserves respect and equal treatment."

- "If you feel discriminated against, report the incident. It is important that all team members feel comfortable and appreciated and that everyone has opportunity here."

- "If someone makes you uncomfortable, tell that person and give him or her an opportunity to change the behavior."

- "I realize some of the women on this team have had prior difficulties with harassment and glass ceilings. The men on this team do not behave that way and deserve respect and cooperation, just as the women do."

- "Everyone on this team should have equal opportunity."

- "Sexual discrimination is unacceptable."

- "It is unacceptable to tell offensive jokes in the office or forward offensive e-mails."

- "If you are unsure of what constitutes offensive language or behavior, err on the side of caution."

- "Just because a woman smiles or plays along, that does not give permission to break our rules of respectful conduct. Some people are embarrassed or fear repercussions if they say something."

- "No one on this team should fear repercussions for speaking out when hearing offensive language or statements."

- "All rules of conduct apply to both men and women."

- "A team is only as strong as the level of respect team members show one another."

- "We are currently investigating a complaint. We want to be clear that harassment complaints from men are taken as seriously as those from women."
- "No one should ever suffer from making a complaint."
- "You might consider what you said a compliment, but be clear that sexual comments are inappropriate here. Reread our sexual harassment guidelines."

Generation Clashes

The Team Mindset

- Four generations share the workplace: the Silent Generation (born 1925–1945), Baby Boomers (born 1946–1964), Generation X (born 1961–1981), and Generation Next (born 1981–2003). (Different sources vary slightly on the years and each generation is known by more than one name; this quick list offers a basic overview.)

- Generational biases and prejudices are counter-productive.

- Within all generations are those who defy the stereotypes of that generation. Avoid making negative stereotypes.

- Some people are still accustomed to the idea that promotions should be based on seniority and feel uncomfortable when younger team members advance quickly or come in at higher levels. Make clear that a younger team member who has received a promotion has the requisite skills, and help set an overall tone of respect for him or her.

- Ensure that all team members, regardless of age, show respect for one another.

- Discourage senior generations' pat responses, such as "We tried that. It didn't work before." An idea may have been before its time; the climate, team knowledge, and technology may allow an old idea new possibilities.

- Discourage junior generations' inclination to blatantly toss out current working processes in favor of new ones.

- Understand that subtle resentments may exist and be sensitive to them, but make the decisions that are best for the team; explain your rationale.
- Respect and learn from the wellspring of experience older team members have to offer; even if times and technology have changed, there is much to be learned from experience.
- Encourage team members to learn from their differences.

Phrases

- "Never underestimate experience."
- "Never underestimate a fresh perspective."
- "We may have tried that before, but this is a new day and a team with fresh perspectives."
- "I realize that you didn't have the same perks when you started in this business, but times have changed and young employees are entering this field with a higher level of specified expertise. Our offers to new hires have to be competitive in order to get the best people for our team."
- "Don't underestimate anyone based on age."
- "Even though Kyle is young, his experience and insight earned him his position on the team."
- "Ava worked here before we were computerized. Her expertise and history with the company are extremely valuable. If she needs extra assistance with our computer systems, it's well worth the effort."
- "If Leon is not comfortable with PowerPoint, let him use his own presentation methods. Since that skill is only useful to him for internal presentations, his time would be best spent preparing the information and learning more essential computer skills."

- "Before we decide how to handle this, let's examine how the problem was handled in the past and consider what worked and what didn't."
- "Before we decide how to handle this, let's get some fresh perspectives."
- "We all have our own generational slang, but let's try to speak the same language."
- "I appreciate the difficulty in having someone so young in our team's rotating leadership program, but she has strong skills and great insight. Give her the same chance you would anyone else."
- "I realize you have a lot of exciting ideas, but be careful not to denigrate the hard work that's come before you."
- "Being exposed to multiple perspectives by the variety of ages on our team is a great advantage."

Discrimination of Any Kind

The Team Mindset

- Never tolerate discrimination based on culture, race, or religion.
- Be versed in sexual harassment and discrimination law. Even if you have others handling such complaints, learn as much as you can and be aware of what is or is not acceptable.
- Act on discrimination claims immediately.
- Never allow racial slurs.
- Don't permit racial jokes.
- Don't encourage, even tacitly, racial jokes.
- Discourage debates over where the line is drawn. Instruct team members to err on the side of extreme caution, and move on.
- Establish clear, effective channels for reporting.
- Never let someone be "punished" for reporting an incident.

Phrases

- "We do not tolerate discrimination."
- "Because of your violation of our discrimination code, I'm sending you to sensitivity training."
- "I'm bringing in a cultural sensitivity expert to help this diverse team work more smoothly together."
- "Racial slurs are not tolerated. You're on warning. The second incident means termination."
- "Racial jokes are not permitted and are a violation of our rules."

- "Please read the team's discrimination laws."
- "I don't care if you *are* [Jewish, Irish, Syrian, etc.]. No one tells racial jokes here."
- "No one should be persecuted for political beliefs here. Politics are not part of our business and should not be discussed in the office. If you choose to take part in a debate, do it after hours."
- "No one should be persecuted for religious beliefs."
- "We have zero tolerance for intolerance!"
- "Thank you for reporting this incident. I will file this report immediately."
- "Thank you for reporting this incident. I need you to file a report with human resources and I will follow up later today to let them know this should be dealt with immediately."

Chapter 5

Empowerment

"When a gifted team dedicates itself to unselfish trust and combines instinct with boldness and effort, it is ready to climb."

—Patanjali

A team only works at full capacity once its members, and the team as a whole, are empowered to make decisions. Empowerment is a process, and expectations should not exceed training. Even simple questions eliciting input from the team empower them and make them feel valued and responsible for positive team outcomes.

Delegation is an empowering act only if you, as the delegator, follow through. Delegation is a process and involves helping team members gain the skills and confidence to do the job, handing over responsibilities, following up on progress, and then letting go.

Listening is part of the act of eliciting input and delegating effectively. One of the most empowering acts, beyond inviting input and delegating, is to listen. Strong teams share ideas, innovations, questions, and concerns—but only when they feel someone is listening.

A Question of Input

The Team Mindset

- Invite input.
- The success of the team depends on your ability to listen.
- Your team members are on the inside, every day, and have knowledge and ideas that they may not readily contribute.
- Create open avenues for team members to contribute and share ideas. Apportion meeting time for new ideas; create message boards online, and consider online discussion groups, where people can sign on to join in a discussion any time.
- Don't fall into the trap of prejudging who the "idea people" are. When you listen openly, you will hear breakout ideas from sources you would have considered the least likely.
- The team input challenge: Team members hold back contributions for any number of reasons: they feel there are no channels; they think that the team leader is already aware of the problem(s); they think that someone must have thought of an idea already; they believe that no one cares or is interested in their opinions. The solution: Ask. Listen.
- Always thank the team or team member for input, even if you cannot use the idea.
- Ask open questions to illicit input. Instead of asking, "Do you agree with the plan?" ask, "What thoughts can you add?" or "What changes would you make to the plan?"
- Create a suggestion box (virtual or real).
- Make a habit of asking and eliciting questions.

➡

Phrases

- "What are your thoughts?"
- "How would you present this idea?"
- "I value your input. Please feel free to chime in any time."
- "I revised the presentation based on comments made by the team. It's stronger now. Thank you for your input."
- "You made an excellent point about the conference location. The arrangements have already been made for this year, but those comments will help us select a better location for next year."
- "Please feel free to revise this method. The tried and true isn't always the best option."
- "Don't hesitate to question me."
- "Questions can be as useful as answers."
- "Let's go around the room so everyone has a chance to offer input."
- "What information does the team need to make this decision?"
- "This decision will affect the future of the company, so I'd like the team's input."
- "This is an important decision, so I would like the team to think through all possible scenarios."
- "I'm holding off my decision until I hear opinions from the team."
- "What changes would you make? Why?"
- "What [additions, modifications, features, recommendations, etc.] would you add?"

The Team Mindset

- You can't possibly do it all.

- Someone else, well trained, may not only prove to be proficient but also demonstrate a creativity that adds immeasurably to the process.

- Delegation—both to the team as a whole and to individuals— is a process.

- Properly trained people will be more successful than those who are thrust forward into new responsibilities "sink-or-swim" style.

- Allowing your team to offer greater contributions lets them participate in important ways and makes them feel that their accomplishments make a difference.

- The more responsibility you give, the greater success your team can achieve.

- Don't make people follow your systems if they prefer their own, which are also effective.

- Provide past examples, templates, and references as options.

- Assure team members that they now "own" the task.

- People will succeed with the confidence to have their own styles, but they also might be more comfortable following established guidelines. Offer a choice.

- If a team member feels passed over by your delegation choices, explain your rationale and say what requirements [skills, timing, etc.] are necessary for the job.

Phrases

- "I have faith in your abilities."
- "I know you can handle this."
- "If you have any questions, please don't hesitate to ask; this is a learning process."
- "I am confident in this team's talent and abilities."
- "Let's set goals and benchmarks together."
- "Do you need additional training?"
- "This is a process. I will be following your progress and stepping back as you grow into the role."
- "I will still have to approve decisions over the next few weeks while you're still learning."
- "I realize you're eager to take over the role and I know you are the right person for this job, but I need to stay involved until your training is complete."
- "You've been doing wonderfully in this role. I'm going to step back completely. I'll still be here if you have questions, but you're in charge of the [team, project, department, etc.] now."
- "I want this client to get to know you. Let's all have lunch so I can introduce you and pass the torch in a relaxed way that will allow her to get to know you."
- "I feel confident entrusting this to you."
- "This project [design, presentation, proposal, etc.] needs your special touch."
- "I'd like you to take this over. I know your expertise [perspective, talents, etc.] will make this fly."
- "I realize you were hoping for this [lead, assignment, role, etc.], but Josie was next in line. This system is the best way to be fair to everyone."

The Team Mindset

- Recruit good people—train them—then trust them.
- Do not delegate then continue to perform the task.
- Once you have delegated, let go. Continuing to hold on undermines the team member when you should be, instead, building confidence and skills and showing trust.
- It's okay to check in to ensure the job is done properly, but don't watch over shoulders.
- As always, praise a job well done. Don't let go without looking back to say, "You did a great job!"
- Ease team members into a change and hand off clients in a way that maintains client comfort and confidence.
- Confirm that the team member is ready for you to let go.
- If a team member you thought was ready lacks confidence, ask why. You may need to offer additional assistance or training.
- Reconcile yourself to the fact that no one is (or should be) a carbon copy of you.
- If your ego is in the way, let it go.

Phrases

- "Are you ready to go out on your own?"
- "I believe you are ready to go out on your own."
- "I'm impressed with what I've seen. I feel fully confident in your abilities."
- "If you have any questions, please don't hesitate to ask. This is a process; you're not expected to know everything the instant you take over this role."
- "This one is all yours."

- "A client from your new territory called me today. I reiterated that you are handling his case now and assured him that you are the best person for the job."

- "I'm not sure where you're headed with that concept, but it's your vision now. I'll let you finish before I comment. I would be happy to give my input if you'd like, but I trust your judgment."

- "I have had this look for a long time, but I'm ready to let this team make some changes. Create a new look that reflects *the team's* personality."

- "This is Christie's project now. Please speak directly to her."

- "Charles is responsible for all issues regarding the new sales initiative. If you have any questions, he's the resident expert now."

- "I'm sorry I sent that e-mail to the board out of habit. You're right. That's your role now and I shouldn't have sent it without speaking to you first."

- "Jackson continues to call me directly because we go so far back. Let me get the two of you together so he can get comfortable with you and see that he's in good hands."

- "If you feel I'm overstepping into the area assigned to you, please point it out to me. It's not my intention."

- "You're right. I assigned this to you and I'm having trouble letting go. It's no reflection on your talent. It's just hard to let go for my own reasons. I'm sorry. I'll back off." *Or* conclude by saying, "I'm sorry, but we need to refine our agreement."

- "I'll be stepping back to let this team function on its own. I'll be here if you need me, but you know your goals, timelines, and team processes. I'll check in with your progress in two weeks."

A Show of Confidence

The Team Mindset

- Offer team members an opportunity to show what they can do.
- If you can let a team member be your representative, introduce that team member in a way that shows your confidence.
- If a team member is not doing well, offer a show of confidence.
- Confidence breeds confidence.
- A team member who feels demeaned will have a hard time gaining confidence.
- Give your team an increasing amount of authority.
- Always speak highly of your team.
- Demonstrate a positive attitude.
- Don't play "devil's advocate" regarding team or team member success.
- Train your team, then give them the freedom to gain confidence in their abilities.

Phrases

- "I would like you to represent us at the conference."
- "You should show this presentation. You have a strong grasp of the concepts and a strong, clear presentation style."
- "I already told Marshall I was bringing in one of my top people. I'll bring you to the next meeting to introduce you."
- "I leave this for the team to decide."

- "Your decision will be final."
- "I *know* you will succeed."
- "I have a good feeling about your success."
- "You have no reason to feel nervous. You are highly skilled and knowledgeable."
- "Would practicing your speech help you feel more confident? This team is a good audience, if you'd like one."
- "You can do it!"
- "Your qualifications are outstanding! No one will question your expertise."
- "Why don't you make the call?"
- "You're doing a fantastic job!"
- "I couldn't have asked for a better team."
- "This one is all yours. Run with it!"

Listening

The Team Mindset

- Instruct and inspire team members to listen to one another.
- If you're too busy to listen, say so and set a time when you can.
- The team cannot function optimally if they do not have strong listening skills.
- As team leader, continually practice improving your listening skills and imparting knowledge to your team.
- Don't let your personal biases interfere with listening.
- Encourage team members to go on; let them know you're listening.
- Don't interrupt.
- Don't finish someone else's sentences.
- Pay attention when team members speak to you. Minimize distractions so that you can focus.
- Encourage notes where it will aid listening and retention.
- Learn more about the importance of listening by visiting the International Listening Association's Web site at Listen.org or by visiting ListenersUnite.com.

Phrases

- "Let's go around the table and give everyone a chance to speak."
- "I'm in a hurry now, but I want to hear what you have to say. Can we talk this afternoon when I get back from my meeting?"
- "What do you think?"

- "What additional thoughts do you have?"
- "I saw you walk by my office before. Did you want to speak with me?"
- "Let's all, as a team, try counting to three before we respond to another team member. It will give us time to really listen to what's being said and be more thoughtful with our responses."
- "I'm listening."
- "Go on."
- "Don't finish one another's sentences."
- "When a team member is speaking in a meeting, no cell phones, computers, or talking—just listen."
- "Feel free to take notes."
- "The most effective way for us to show our respect for one another is to listen."
- "I realize you're excited about your ideas, but please listen first."
- "I want to listen to everyone, so we cannot all speak at once."
- "Listen."

Chapter 6

Feedback

"It is literally true that you can succeed best and quickest by helping others to succeed."

—Napoleon Hill

Without feedback, it is impossible for team members to know that they are meeting expectations. Giving feedback—both positive and developmental—is one of the team leader's most important tasks. Positive feedback keeps the team motivated, while developmental feedback keeps everyone on track and clued in to exactly what is expected.

Feedback should be encouraged from every direction: from team leaders, self-assessment, team members, clients, and customers. In fact, you may alter your view of a team member by hearing the frustrations and praise of those within the team and those on the consumer, user, or client side.

Feedback avenues might include both formal, written forms (with ranking systems and/or open questions); feedback discussions, both as a group and/or privately with the team leader; and informal meeting questions.

Job Coaching

The Team Mindset

- Providing guidance and encouragement is essential to the team leader's role.

- Job coaching should be an ongoing process, not a one-time meeting.

- Performance appraisals are only one part of job coaching, which should be an endless loop of feedback and follow-up.

- No one can do a good job if expectations and goals are not clearly defined.

- Specific, timely feedback gets results; vague statements made a week later won't have the same impact.

- Watch your language and tone. Don't unnecessarily put someone in a defensive mode. Defensiveness shuts down listening.

- Do not hesitate to give developmental feedback when necessary. In the end, it helps both the individual and the team.

- Don't ignore troubling behaviors or errors in an effort to be "nice," then reprimand when the problem continues. Problems don't resolve themselves, and team members won't know they're missing the mark if you don't tell them.

- It's easy to take good work for granted. Make time for specific, timely, positive feedback.

- When you present a behavior that must be changed, don't use the "because I said so" stance; clearly state the impact that behavior has on the team.

➡

- Feedback that requires change should always be followed up with encouragement, praise, additional suggestions, and asking the feedback recipient for his or her own assessment of the change. Invite questions regarding the change process.

Phrases

- "I like the way you handled that [situation, problem, account, etc.]."
- "I'm impressed with the creativity you showed on this project. Would you share your insights with the team?"
- "When you're in the field, it's important for you to be reachable. When Jay and Hanna needed your approval yesterday and couldn't reach you, the whole job was tied up."
- "I received a glowing client e-mail about your above-and-beyond service. I forwarded it to you *and* to corporate. Keep up the great work!"
- "I realize you have been bombarded with complaints and I can see that it would be impossible for you to keep everyone happy with your workload. I'm sorry you have had to take the brunt of customer frustrations. I plan to make changes and hire another team member."
- "We have been receiving a number of complaints about efficiency. Orders are slow and phones go unanswered. Do you have ideas about how to run things more smoothly?"
- "This morning, I saw a client storming away angrily. What happened?"
- "Let's celebrate what's good—what's working—and also take a look at some areas we may need to strengthen."

- "Please report any misconduct that affects team member process or morale."
- "I realize that you're accustomed to your way of doing things, but I would appreciate it if you would give this new system a try. Beyond the learning curve—which won't take long for you—other team members are reporting greater efficiency."
- "I know that you want to help the team, but harsh criticism of other team members hurts morale. Please follow our feedback guidelines. Be specific in your phrasing, know when to let the less important points go, and add something positive."
- "I would like to recommend you for training in the new software system during our trial period. I think you have great capabilities, so you can be our pioneer in this area and let the rest of us know if you think it's worth the investment."
- "How would you suggest we handle these complaints?"
- "This team seems to be floundering. We have a lot of projects going, but none has reached completion by the schedule we set earlier this year. What do you think the problem is? What remedies do you suggest?"
- "Let's meet to review your progress in the areas we discussed. From what I can see, you're doing quite well!"
- "How well are you able to implement the changes we spoke about? Do you have any questions or concerns?"

The Team Mindset

- Team assessments should be conducted in a structured, positive way.
- Be careful not to create an environment where assessments are associated with criticism.
- Team members should not be admonished by other members of the team.
- Feedback is most effective when provided in a supportive atmosphere.
- Team member interactions, such as e-mail messages and phone recordings, should only be shared with that team member's prior knowledge and permission.
- Create a system whereby suggestions made by one team member to another are accompanied by a specific statement of praise or appreciation.
- Encourage praise.
- If one team member comes to you with a complaint about another team member, hear the other side privately, and then speak to both people together to resolve the issue.
- Ask team members specific questions, but also ask them to rate the overall team.
- As always, follow up to ensure that team members' critiques and suggestions are considered. Address complaints and then check with team members to ensure that the solution meets their needs. In addition, ideas that are accepted should be implemented and become part of the team process.

➡

- If these ideas fall through the cracks, so will morale. Also, any future attempt to elicit suggestions from the team will be seen as false efforts and empty promises. Build on the good suggestions you receive; find time to follow through.

Phrases

- "On a scale of 1 to 10, how would you rate this team's spirit? What would you suggest to raise that rating?"
- "Let's assess what went wrong in this case. Then, I want to hear ideas from you as to how to avoid these problems next time."
- "Is everyone's input encouraged and respected?"
- "What is the process for conflict resolution? Is it working?"
- "Does the team follow established structures?"
- "Is there any recurring or ongoing problem with team processes? Do you have any suggestions? Let's put this problem to the team to brainstorm solutions."
- "Is every necessary role covered? What issues [problems, situations, etc.] fall through the cracks?"
- "Is there overlap of responsibilities? If so, is it working as a back-up system or causing confusion and duplicated efforts?"
- "What, in your view, is the team's greatest asset?"
- "What, in your view, is the team's greatest challenge?"
- "Does the team consistently move toward established goals?"
- "Do you consider this team to have adequate support systems?"
- "What is working well on the team? What isn't?"

➡

- "Are your talents being fully utilized by the team?"
- "Do you feel confident in your position on the team?"
- "Do you feel respected by your team members?"
- "Do you and your team members handle conflict in a constructive, professional manner?"

Team Member Self-Assessments

The Team Mindset

- Team member self-assessments are valuable exercises.

- Team member self-assessments provide interesting insights, especially when compared with others' assessments of the same team member. What matches? What doesn't? What perceptions may be tainted by past events or outside influences?

- People are often reticent to toot their own horns; encourage honest, positive self-assessment, which can provide useful knowledge as you assign tasks. Encourage "bragging" when "bragging rights" have been earned.

- Asking the right questions will remind team members of the importance of team behaviors, like pitching in when a team member needs help.

- A question can be suggestive in a positive way, such as, "If you don't have time to help a team member, do you take a moment to refer someone else who might help?"

- Questions with embedded answers can be helpful for quick, simple, recurring self-assessments. But ideally, ask open questions that allow the team member to explore past behavior or find his or her own solutions.

- Self-assessments may either be given in a group setting or to team members to fill out on their own, within a specified time frame. Assessments may be reviewed with the team leader and relevant aspects reviewed with the team.

- Sensitive self-assessment responses must remain private. Assure team members that their privacy will be

➡

respected and let them know that no self-assessment answers will be shared without permission.
- Ask questions relating to both assets and shortcomings regarding technical and communication skills.
- Follow up.

Phrases

- "How would you rate your performance?"
- "How would you rate your ability to fulfill your role on the team?"
- "What assets do you bring to the team?"
- "What changes would you like to make that would strengthen your role on the team?"
- "What talents do you have that you are not using that you feel would be beneficial to the team?"
- "How would you imagine team members would describe you? Would you agree?"
- "I know you're modest, but please don't hesitate to talk about your strengths, too. There may be things I don't see and, when other opportunities arise, I should know all I can about your capabilities and accomplishments."
- "List three of your positive attributes that are assets to the team."
- "What skills would you like to improve that would help you in your role on the team?"
- "What challenges do you find? What ideas do you have for overcoming them? What do you need from me? What do you need from the team?"
- "Think of an incident that turned out well. What did you do right? Would you have done anything differently if you had it to do again?"

- "Think of an incident that didn't turn out well. What went wrong? What was your role in the problem? What would you do differently next time?"
- "Do you consider yourself a team player? What criticisms have you heard from the team? Is there any validity to the claims?"
- "What changes can you make to become a stronger team player?"
- "How do you typically respond when a team member needs your assistance?"
- "If a team member requests assistance when you don't have time to help, do you take a moment to make suggestions about where to find solutions or who else might be able to help?"
- "Do you consider yourself a good listener? Why or why not?"

Feedback Among Team Members

The Team Mindset

- Encourage team members to use positive language.
- Set a standard for team member feedback that requires stating the reason for the feedback or team benefit behind the suggestion.
- Teams must understand the principles of using descriptive language rather than vague criticisms. Teach and model this important communication skill.
- Team members who have an opportunity to assess other team members' performances and the team as a whole will have a stronger understanding of the team process and everyone's roles.
- While positive feedback should be welcome at all times in all forms, hold team members to feedback conduct guidelines when delicate matters are involved. Feedback should be timely and based on facts, not generalizations.
- Generating positive feedback among team members will fuel individual confidence.
- Personality clashes should have no bearing on performance critique.
- The purpose of critiquing team members is to strengthen the team and help team members reach their full potential.
- Criticism must be *specific* and *timely*.
- Encourage praise—*always*.

Phrases

- "This team feedback should be done with an eye toward building up the team, not knocking anyone down."

- "I understand that you feel Kim is uncooperative, but can you tell her how? I'm sure that she wants to be cooperative, and we can only improve ourselves if we have a clear understanding of the problem. Please use specific examples."
- "Name calling is worse than pointless; it is detrimental to the spirit of the team."
- "Never tell someone *you never* or *you always*. Neither is always true."
- "If you have a problem with another team member's action, speak to that person privately."
- "A client should never hear one team member criticizing another."
- "If a team member undermines your image with a customer, don't get defensive or aggressive. Let it go until you can speak privately, then offer a simple reminder that undercutting your image hurts the team."
- "One of the great assets of a team is that we can learn from each other."
- "Give and accept feedback in the spirit of learning and helping each other achieve greater success."
- "I'd like everyone here to say something positive about the person sitting to your right."
- "Team feedback is a source of support and growth, not criticism."
- "Resist the urge to be defensive."
- "Listen carefully to team member critiques."
- "Understand that all critiques are offered in the spirit of strengthening the team and helping team members grow and succeed."
- "We can all use some outside perspective."

Assessments of the Team Leader

The Team Mindset

- No one is perfect—even exceptionally talented, well-intentioned team leaders—so encourage feedback from your team.

- By encouraging your team to critique your work and openly give feedback and suggestions, you will show that you respect their opinions.

- When a good suggestion comes along, take it. At least make the effort and show that you are.

- You might be getting in the way of progress without realizing it.

- You could be unwittingly demotivating someone with words or actions you thought would motivate.

- Be public about your goals for change. It is always encouraging to see someone take on personal or professional improvement plans. Doing so will inspire team members who are working to make changes based on developmental feedback.

- If you make a change, credit and thank the source.

- You will inevitably learn something about yourself by listening openly to other perspectives.

- Share your own self-assessment and be forthcoming about ways you intend to improve to help the team (e.g., better cell phone service and being early for meetings).

- Anonymous feedback protocols open a channel for raw, honest critiques of the team leader.

Phrases

- "How am I doing? Please be honest. There will be no repercussions."
- "What do you need from me that you don't get?"
- "What do I do that's positive and encouraging?"
- "What do I do that feels like it is slowing down progress?"
- "Do you feel that your talent is appreciated?"
- "What can I do to make everyone on this team feel appreciated?"
- "Do you feel that your skills and abilities are being used?"
- "What would you change about your working situation?"
- "If you were in my position, what would you do differently?"
- "Are your concerns addressed to your satisfaction? Why or why not?"
- "My poor memory seems to cause a lot of last-minute flustered rushing. I realize this, and I'm working on it. If anyone has an organizational or memory tip, I'm open to suggestions."
- "Like everyone else on this team, I want to give my all and do the best that I can. I take your feedback very seriously."
- "I respect your opinions and value your feedback."
- "I expect to be held as accountable as anyone else for making positive changes."
- "You're right. Thank you for pointing that out."

The Little Things

The Team Mindset

- Some little things have a tremendous impact, like the little phrases in this section.
- Small phrases, which may seem trite at first glance, are powerful and often underused.
- Make these essential phrases a part of your vocabulary and use them without hesitation.
- Seemingly small gestures, such as encouraging e-mails, even a line or two, show appreciation.
- A hand-written note is a rarity that shows you put in extra effort to demonstrate your genuine appreciation.
- Admitting when you are wrong shows strength and insight, not weakness.
- Ask people's opinions, even when you think you've got it all figured out.
- Be thankful for the good people around you—and let them know it. It's their work that makes you look good.
- A cheerful, good-spirited greeting sets an upbeat tone for the day.
- The expectations you have of someone who always does a good job, always has your back, and rolls along with rarely a squeak, may keep you from verbalizing your appreciation—don't let them. You surely don't want such a valuable team member to feel unappreciated.

Phrases

- "Good morning!"
- "How was your weekend?"

- "You were right."
- "I was wrong."
- "I'm sorry."
- "What do you think?"
- "Why?"
- "What do you need from me?"
- "Great job!"
- "Nicely done!"
- "You are *always* there, *always* with just what is needed! Thank you!"
- "I don't know what I would do without you."
- "This is my dream team—I couldn't have asked for better!"
- "I couldn't have done it without you."
- "Thank you."
- That last one bears repeating, as it should be repeated often: "Thank you."

Chapter 7

Team Process

"If you give people tools, [and they use] their natural ability and their curiosity, they will develop things in a way that will surprise you very much beyond what you might have expected."

—Bill Gates

Strong teams work with a number of tools. By using a variety of processes well and being open to trying others, the team keeps thinking creatively. Brainstorming, creative thinking, and problem solving are all essential team processes, which can be implemented in various ways and used to spring off a number of more complex processes. However, even with only these simple tools, a strong team can achieve great success.

All processes that elicit ideas should be followed with action plans. The last section in this chapter suggests some thoughts for action planning. Use any one or a combination of the following processes, build on them, and use some form of action planning to ensure that good ideas don't get lost. Your team will feel disempowered if they work hard to find ideas or solutions that are erased from a whiteboard and forgotten. Help your team with processes and follow-throughs that will help them succeed.

Brainstorming

The Team Mindset

- Brainstorming fits in with a number of creative processes.
- Even team members who work in different time zones can take part in online brainstorming.
- Brainstorming can be done in a room or online, but the two methods will have a very different energy. Opt to have your team in one room, if possible.
- The brainstorming process is more than throwing out ideas. The team must record, review, prioritize, and put those ideas into an action plan.
- Ideas that are valuable but not immediately viable should be filed in such a way that they can be easily retrieved and not forgotten.
- Online discussion groups create a rolling brainstorm session. Be clear that no other topic should be discussed within the same subject heading; other topics should be sent separately with their own specific subject lines.
- Continue brainstorming for another five or ten minutes after everyone has run out of ideas—there is always more to come.
- Don't immediately discount anything.
- All ideas should be recorded.
- Brainstorming is only effective when it leads to a team-created, time-framed action plan.

Phrases

- "There are no wrong answers."
- "All ideas are welcome."

- "Please, no critique of or reaction to ideas at this stage. We are just looking to get a flow of ideas."
- "Often, the most interesting ideas come once we think we've exhausted all reasonable possibilities."
- "Now that we have a number of great ideas, let's narrow them down. What's feasible?"
- "How would you, as a team, suggest prioritizing?"
- "Let's create an action plan based on this session. We don't want to lose any of these ideas."
- "It's important to establish realistic time frames for action plans and stick to them. You tell me—what's possible?"
- "Our deadline is August 3, but let's set an internal deadline of July 15. We all know how last-minute issues arise."
- "Great planning. Let's put it in motion!"
- "Let's break into teams for this exercise. How many uses can you think of for a ballpoint pen? You have ten minutes. When you think you've thought of everything, keep going. The team with the most uses at the end wins the game."
- "We have some great ideas here. Now let's determine which are most viable in the current climate."
- "Now it's time to create a time-framed action plan."
- "We've collected, in our team assessments, everyone's view of the team's greatest challenge. Let's look at each and brainstorm solutions."
- "Of the team solutions we've brainstormed, what works? What doesn't? Work as a team to create new systems and action plans to solve these issues and make this team even stronger."

Creative Thinking

The Team Mindset

- Not everyone has the same creative process. Allow for a variety of creative process styles.
- Leave time for creative thinking.
- Put out an issue and give people time to think about it. Ideas often pop up at the oddest times, usually when we've stopped concentrating.
- Suggest that people take a brief break to recharge.
- Offer recharging suggestions, such as meditation, creative imagery, walking, or stretching.
- Urge people not to use their recharge break to be on the phone or checking e-mails, but really to step back from the day to come back refreshed.
- Run a midmorning group stretching session.
- Hold meetings with the sole purpose of generating creative ideas. Be clear that implementation may not be immediate, but don't let good ideas disappear. Keep track of creative notions that arise during these meetings.
- Allow people to express their own creative styles in the workspace and in the work itself.
- Give brief thinking exercises at the opening of a meeting, a day, or a week, just to get people's brains facile and ready to go.
- Reverse a process to loosen up thinking. Breaking structure lets loose creative thinking.
- Try putting two seemingly unrelated items or ideas side by side (physically or figuratively) and having the team find connections.

Phrases

- "Even the most innovative improvements can be built upon."

- "Never be afraid to speak out with a 'crazy' idea. This team favors nonconformity over conformity."

- "Don't be held back by fear of failure. Even failed experiments teach us something. At the very least, they teach us what won't work."

- "As much as we know, there is an infinite amount that we do not, and curiosity leads to creativity."

- "Even if something is working, new levels may be achieved by new thinking."

- "Let's take a ten-minute break to recharge."

- "We can learn from each other's creative processes. Does anyone have a tip or method to share?"

- "I'm going to take responses and ideas now, then meet again in the morning to see what additional ideas come up after we've all had a night to sleep on it."

- "I suggest using the afternoon break for meditation, creative imagery, fresh air—anything that recharges your creative battery."

- "I urge you not to work through the break; you will come back stronger and the time you put in will be more productive."

- "Please join us for the midmorning stretch."

- "Let's turn our meeting schedule upside down and run it backwards today."

- "What connections can you find between our customer service initiative and our team's ground rules?"

- "Think about the products you've seen in your lifetime. What has had the most unforgettably creative marketing strategy? Why?"
- "We worked hard on our latest proposal. Who else might be interested in that same proposal with the fewest modifications? Let's brainstorm a target list."

Problem Solving

The Team Mindset

- Trial and error is one problem-solving process. Depending on scope and practical issues, you can run through a process from beginning to end either in practice or theoretically.

- Examining the causes is often necessary to find and implement solutions and prevent recurrences of the issue. However, there are instances where the cause is unimportant and searching for causes detracts from the goal. In these cases, choose solution-oriented problem solving.

- When time is a factor, problem solving will have to move forward when the team might otherwise spend more time generating solutions. Alter processes based on available time and resources.

- Identify and challenge assumptions.

- Examine alternative scenarios.

- Gather as many different perspectives as you can.

- A complex problem may hold its own solution if your team takes time to dissect and understand it.

- The central problem, itself, may be masked by symptoms or other problems. Dig down and get to the real problem.

- Acknowledging that the team doesn't already have the best solution is the most significant step toward finding it.

- Evaluate possible complex solutions with a cost/benefit analysis.

➡

Phrases

- "Every problem comes with a few solutions. We just have to find them."
- "Start thinking of challenges as opportunities."
- "If we start looking at problems as roadblocks, we won't get around them. It's creative thinking that will help us find another way and we have extremely creative thinkers here."
- "What assumptions do we have going in? Are they valid? What objections do they raise and what possible solutions can we find?"
- "How many alternative scenarios can we imagine?"
- "We can come to agreements later. But, for now, I want to hear as many divergent perspectives as we can come up with."
- "Delving in to understand the problem more carefully might just reveal the solution."
- "Problems always contain hidden opportunities."
- "The quality of the questions we ask will determine the quality of our solutions."
- "Let's be careful to solve the problem, not just alleviate the symptoms."
- "Admitting we don't know the answer is the first step toward finding a viable one."
- "Now, let's run each of these possible solutions through a cost/benefit analysis."
- "Now that we have a number of possible solutions, which are the most viable? Have we found the best solution yet?"
- "We are running out of time. Which, of these possible solutions, is the best option?"
- "What would the simple solution be? Is it really *too* simple, or are we overcomplicating the issue?"

Decision Making

The Team Mindset

- Team decision making is more challenging than making individual decisions.

- Team decision making requires all team members to hone the skills of negotiation, listening, and compromise.

- The quality of a decision cannot be determined solely by the outcome. A good decision can encounter unforeseeable events.

- Good decisions do not guarantee success; they increase probability.

- Computer programs can assist in decision making with high-powered three-dimensional visualization and display graphics and simulation techniques.

- Decision making requires accurate, up-to-date information.

- If a decision leads to a long-term process, set checkpoints for reevaluation and possible changes in direction.

- What happens if everything goes wrong? For major decisions, have the team consider the worst-case scenario. Doing so will help them best assess risks and possibly take bolder steps if it determines that the worst-case scenario is not as bad as initially thought.

- For major decisions, try to reach a consensus among team members. If one cannot easily be reached, consider how the decision can be altered in a way that will maintain its overall integrity but bring the rest of the team on board.

- Try assigning some team members to play "devil's advocate," questioning every aspect of a proposed decision. This is an important exercise. Even if team members agree, they must do their part to bring out the potential negative points so the team can consider, discuss, and potentially overcome them.

Phrases

- "Which team members would like to play devil's advocate? We'll need you to raise every possible objection. Please don't hold back, even if you support the decision. This process will help us find and strengthen weaknesses."
- "We cannot make a decision without establishing that we're working with the latest data. Has anyone confirmed that we are working with the most up-to-date figures?"
- "The outcome didn't go well, but it was still a good, solid decision based on the facts we had and reasonable predictions."
- "What's the worst-case scenario?"
- "What will it take to reach a consensus on this?"
- "For this decision, we will have to go with the majority vote."
- "What computer programs do we have that will assist in this process?"
- "Can we run through a few 'what-if' scenarios?"
- "Let's set up a virtual simulation to view possible outcomes."
- "It is important to the team to get everyone's input."
- "Let's go with this decision, but establish some checkpoints along the way. We want to remain flexible."
- "What are the pros?"

- "What are the cons?"
- "Does anyone have concerns going forward?"
- "No one can guarantee the correctness of a decision because no one can see into the future."
- "What worked well about the decision-making process we used today?"

Action Plans

The Team Mindset

- Teams will develop new goals as a result of brainstorming.
- The team must work these goals into the framework of timelines.
- A team that develops action plans will be more invested in the process than a team that has action plans handed to them.
- Restate the goal, in writing, for your team to see as they develop action plans.
- A team's multiple action plans must not interfere with each other.
- If a new action plan conflicts with an old one, consider revising the old as readily as refining the new.
- The team must determine who is responsible for which actions.
- Established time frames are essential for solid action plans.
- Team members must come to some consensus about priorities in order to create and carry out action plans.
- Ensure that the action plan is clear to everyone.

Phrases

- "As a result of our brainstorming, we have established new goals. We need to develop action plans and put those goals into the context of the rest of our work."
- "Of those which we decided to pursue, which is the most important?"
- "What needs to be done?"
- "Who, on the team, will take these actions?"

- "What would success look like?"
- "What outside sources or information are necessary to achieve these goals?"
- "Who here has access to the sources and information necessary to achieve these goals?"
- "What is the time frame for the overall goal?"
- "Let's establish time frames for each of the interim steps identified."
- "What resistance might we encounter in carrying out this action plan?"
- "What can we do to minimize obstacles?"
- "Who else needs to know about the plan?"
- "Is this action plan clear to everyone?"

Implementation

A Team Mindset

- If plans are not implemented, brainstorming, goal setting, and action planning come to nothing but wasted time. It is also demoralizing for a team to work toward an end that is suddenly dropped. Don't make directional shifts lightly, especially once the team has worked hard.
- Implementation may seem simple, but integrating new decisions and goals into a long-range plan is a complex process.
- Implementation is where your team really needs to come together.
- Implementation of major ideas and initiatives may happen over time and involve intense team synergy.
- Implementation is covered in most every section of this book; it is the daily work of your team.
- Your team should refer to its action plans throughout the implementation process. Plans should not be kept in a drawer or posted in a forgotten place with phone messages scrawled on them.
- Team members should work the plan, but not be so attached that they are unwilling or unable to change directions if necessary.
- Once a decision has been made, the team needs to move beyond debate and come together as a team to move forward with the plan.

Phrases

- "Are we on schedule?"
- "What challenges are we facing as we go forward?"

➥

- "Does anyone have any questions, now that we've begun the process?"
- "It's time to reevaluate. Are we heading in the right direction?"
- "What has changed since the plan's implementation that would impact the intended outcome?"
- "Is anyone hitting snags in the implementation process? What can the team do to help?"
- "I realize that you were not behind this decision, but we are in the process now and our success relies on your efforts as much as on those of anyone else on the team."
- "I'll need everyone's progress report to ensure that the team is on target and moving forward."
- "Please include a 'Challenges' section in your report to let the team know what challenges you face in your role, so we can help."
- "Reports can be short and sweet but must cover all of the relevant points of our standard headings."
- "Is the process working as smoothly as we had hoped?"
- "Looking back, did we make the right decision?"
- "Let's play 'Monday morning quarterback' so that we can assess the process and consider where we might have seen some of these obstacles at an earlier stage."
- "Great job, everyone! The process is in full swing and we are all on target."

Chapter 8

Virtual Team Building

"I'm very proud of my team. I'm just glad they're somewhere else (because I'm in my underwear)."

—Ray Villarosa

Working from home has its advantages. But whether
your team is entirely or partially virtual, team success
may depend on your familiarity and comfort with a
number of communication methods and options. Even if your
team works entirely in one space, understanding these options
may help you provide incentives or make a change necessary
to keep a valued team member on board. Keep in mind that
whatever you learn this month may be different next month
and that methods for virtual team building are expanding at
the rate of technology.

If you're not an expert, hire one. Don't be caught up in
keeping up, but keep an ear out or check in from time to time
to see if some available option would help your team. As you
build and enhance virtual teams, keep in mind that team building should never fall away to be lost somewhere in cyberspace.
If ever a team needs building and extra efforts aimed toward
cohesion, it's a team who works at a distance.

Off-Site Team Leader

The Team Mindset

- Even if you are not in the next office, be as accessible as possible.
- Be reachable. Team members need to know how best to reach you at different times of the day.
- Return calls or check e-mails as often and as quickly as you can.
- Make yourself available through instant messaging. If you find that IM is a distraction, you might designate certain times that you are available or will be online.
- Be timely in returning team member inquiries.
- Technology enables strong off-site management, which comes in handy when you establish more than one physical office, but do not underestimate face time. Even if you hire an on-site manager, visit individual offices and people.
- As an off-site team leader, check in and be available using more than one method of communication.
- Video conferencing can "put you in the room." Your presence will have more of an impact than a phone call.
- Use message and discussion boards, conferencing software, and cell phones to keep in touch with your team.
- Ask for feedback on the process and be open to making changes.

Phrases

- "Please do not hesitate to call me if you have questions."
- "I will be online every morning from nine to ten."

- "If you have a question and I am not available by cell phone, please leave a message. I check in regularly."
- "I realize that our situation can be challenging. Let's work together to keep this operation running smoothly."
- "I will come into the office for two meetings per month, but we will also schedule regular phone conferences. Please don't hesitate to call or write with any questions in the meantime."
- "I may be off-site, but I'm only a phone call away."
- "I am providing videoconferencing equipment for interim discussions, but I will still fly in for our scheduled meetings. If, for some reason, I can't be here, we will use this system as backup."
- "I have set up an online discussion board so that I can have ongoing 'conversations' with the team."
- "If you need to make a decision to move forward on something you would normally clear with me, leave detailed messages and use your best judgment if I don't respond in time."
- "I will have my travel schedule, availability, and in-office visits posted on my online calendar."
- "Please keep the team calendar up to date. Even if the team is aware of minor changes, I would like to know what's happening."
- "I will check in with the discussion board and e-mails at the beginning and end of each day. If you need to reach me in the interim, please call my cell phone."
- "I'm lucky to have such a great team! It makes my job so much easier to know that the team can operate smoothly when I'm not here."

➡

- "This arrangement wouldn't work if we didn't have such a strong team. Thanks for your dedication and flexibility!"
- "If any part of this virtual team process is not working well for you, please bring that to my attention and we'll see what adjustments we can make."
- "In my absence, I want to create a system of rotating leadership. The interim leader will stay connected with me and will be in charge when I can't be reached."

Off-Site Team Member

The Team Mindset

- When most of your team is on-site, remember that those who work off-site are also part of the team and it is important for them to feel that way.
- Be sure to have on-site team members treat off-site team members as part of the team.
- While it is an extra effort to keep off-site employees informed, take it seriously—for big things and small.
- Invite off-site members to on-site events; if attendance is not possible, those members should still be informed.
- Keep off-site team members up to speed technologically, providing equipment that will help them do their jobs.
- Be clear as to what is important to you: being accessible during business hours, message turnaround time, etc.
- Remember off-site team members for perks or special assignments. Beware of adopting an "out-of-site," out-of-mind mentality.
- Send items with company logos to give an in-office feel to those working at home or in satellite locations.
- Arrange, if possible, for off-site team members to come in for periodic in-office visits and events.
- Include off-site employees in meetings via conference calls.

Phrases

- "What do you need that will help you do your job better?"
- "You are an important part of the team. Please let me and other team members know what we can do to help make this work for you."

- "Sandra is no less a part of our team because she works outside of the office."

- "Who would like to be Paolo's liaison in the office? We need one person to be responsible for forwarding him information beyond reports posted online."

- "Please join our Monday morning meetings. If you can't come in, we can set up a conference call."

- "When you post Jenna's picture online as Employee of the Month, please also post the picture on our office bulletin board, the way we would for any team member. We can e-mail a snapshot to show her she gets the same honors as every other winner."

- "Attached is our logo, in case you want to use it as wallpaper for your cyber–home office."

- "We just upgraded our software in the office. Attached is your upgrade. Please call if you have any problems installing it. I think you'll enjoy the new features!"

- "I noticed you're not chiming in on the discussion boards. I hope you realize the team values your opinion. The last item discussed led to an informal survey. We would all like to know your opinions."

- "Are you getting everything you need from the team?"

- "Are you getting everything you need from me?"

- "I'm glad we tried this virtual arrangement. We didn't want to lose you when you moved!"

- "If you prefer to work on weekends and take weekdays off, that's fine. I'm more concerned with output than time frames. However, I do need you to be accessible by cell phone during business hours."

➡

- "How is it going working from home? I realize it's a big transition. It's a change for all of us. Please let us know how we can help this run as smoothly as possible for you."
- "If any part of this distance working process is not working well for you, please bring that to my attention and we'll see what adjustments we can make."

The Virtual Team

The Team Mindset

- Don't hold one team's standards and processes up to another's. What has worked for one virtual team may not work for another.

- Understand that some in-office processes work for the virtual team while others do not. Listen to your team to learn what is or is not working.

- Take advantage of all technical avenues that will increase communication.

- Create clear guidelines and expectations for use of and responses to discussion boards, e-mails, voice mails, and pages.

- Do what you can to add personality to technical communications. Personalized icons, photographs, voice, and video all add a personal element.

- If you are transitioning from an on-site team to a virtual one, consider transitioning team processes that work in the physical boardroom and altering them to accommodate virtual communications.

- Virtual team communication methods are continually being refined.

- Join organizations and find online resources for virtual team leaders.

- Even terminology is emerging. One work-at-home entrepreneur coined the title CHO, Chief Home Officer. You can find his articles and blog on virtual teams at chiefhomeofficer.com.

➡

- Keep up to date on emerging collaboration software. Teams can share desktops and files at a distance, and software is continually emerging and improving.

Phrases

- "E-mail, instant messages, and phone and voice mail all have their own advantages. Choose the best medium for the message."
- "With all of the technology options, don't neglect the importance of hearing a voice once in a while. Much can be told from a tone of voice and gained from a more human connection."
- "Our new software will allow us new file sharing and team editing capabilities."
- "I want everyone's pictures posted so we can see who we're 'talking' to."
- "Working online makes our written communications especially important. I have ordered an online business writing seminar for all team members."
- "I need everyone up to speed on the new collaborative software."
- "I don't see the same level of work I saw when you were in the office. What can we do to make this work smoothly?"
- "What problems are you encountering with our virtual communication systems? How could we run this operation more smoothly?"
- "We have a new virtual receptionist to streamline calls coming in for team members. I have e-mailed everyone instructions on checking messages along with a detailed account of how the company was instructed to answer our calls."

- "We have a new virtual receptionist who can answer simple questions before forwarding calls to us. Let's work together to determine what information we should make available to potential customers through this system."

- "Before we try the online conference system with clients, let's hold a meeting online to see how well the system works."

- "Tone is hard to read in e-mails. Assume the best intentions of teammates."

- "We all get a lot of e-mails and often save key information in e-mail files. Let's make it easy for each other with specific subject lines."

- "Instant messaging is useful, but overuse causes distraction for many of us. Please refrain from overusing it."

- "Use instant messaging protocols. Start by asking if the recipient is busy or has a minute for a quick exchange."

- "If you're instant messaging and you get a phone call, signal that you'll be right back. Follow basic courtesies."

Across Time Zones

The Team Mindset

- Working across time zones has its challenges, but it has become so common that there is no shortage of resources available to assist you and your national or global team.

- Online access allows people to work together on rotating schedules.

- Discussion boards create what is known as a "rolling discussion," where people can chime in to the exchange and post thoughts in their own time.

- Keep all team member clocks and calendars in mind when making plans and setting deadlines.

- If you have teams working in a physical office, keep clocks on the wall set to all team member locations.

- Where possible, building in an extra cushion of time is especially important.

- When launching your project or business, arrange, if possible, for team members to meet in one place so that people can meet face to face.

- Team calendars should include cross-cultural holidays. Encourage team members to put these special dates or holidays on their own calendars so that they can be respectful of others and work around important dates.

- When team members make time-based requests or give deadlines, ask them to be clear in specifying "your time" or "our time."

- Bring in a cultural/language specialist to give cross-cultural insights and answer questions.

➡

Phrases

- "Keep in mind that we only have until two o'clock, our time, to get this to the rest of the team so they will have it before the end of their workday."

- "Build in extra time for scheduling because, with the time difference, there is more room for something to go wrong on one end while the other end is sleeping."

- "That e-mail might have seemed [rude, overly friendly, unprofessional, etc.] to you, but the reason behind that is not bad intention or lack of respect; it's simply a cultural difference."

- "I have arranged for a language and cultural specialist to come in and talk to us about cultural differences to help us understand and better communicate with team members and clients."

- "Our cultural expert is coming in again. I'd like everyone to think about questions or challenging situations in advance."

- "When scheduling, take all team member time zones into account."

- "Reach out to the customer account manager first when scheduling the phone conference. Because she is overseas, we will all have to work around her schedule."

- "Please check dates carefully to avoid scheduling something on a date that infringes on anyone's important holidays."

- "We are flying in your European team members to celebrate this success and launch the next initiative."

- "We will rotate our annual 'team meet' between here and California so that everyone on the team only has to travel once every two years."

- "The seminar will be at 10 a.m. our time. Please post the time for both time zones in the meeting invitation."

- "Before completing our Spanish campaign, run it by a cultural expert. We don't know if the direct translation or symbols we use have some other meaning there."

- "Just looking at the Jewish calendar won't tell you which holidays are important for days off. Many of the minor holidays are not typically days off. Check with a team member to ensure that you're working around important holidays."

- "I understand that you didn't realize it was Good Friday when you scheduled the meeting. We'll need to apologize for the error and reschedule."

- "Sometimes we take a team member's style as rude or brusque when it's more of a cultural style. Always assume the best intentions of team members and try to understand common cultural styles."

On-the-Clock vs. Results-Only Hours

The Team Mindset

■ Some team leaders don't care how much time individual team members put in, as long as very specific results are achieved. Results-only management works well as long as the quality and quantity of work are consistently up to established standards.

■ Some team leaders feel strongly that team members work for an agreed-upon number of hours, but leave the timing of those hours (day or evening, weekday or weekend) to the individuals.

■ Even if the specific hours don't matter, it may be important to have team members available during specified hours. Create a system that works for you, your team, and your clients.

■ Some teams operate best when everyone is working the same hours at the same time, with no question of accessibility.

■ As a team leader, think of what kind of schedule works best for your team. No option is wrong. Consider both the nature of your work, the needs of your clients and associates, and how you believe you and your team members will function optimally.

■ Instead of choosing what is most familiar, choose what will work well for and motivate your team.

■ Many people are highly motivated by flexible hours.

■ Salary and bonuses may be less important than the freedom afforded by a flexible schedule.

➡

- Team members, depending on their roles, may put in different hours or be required to be available during certain times. Make sure that team members know one another's schedules, and be clear that those schedules are determined by team functions, not preferential treatment.
- If you agree on a system that isn't working well, meet with the team member or team members to revise the system; give it time. If an arrangement isn't working and needs to be changed, give adequate warning and team members ample opportunity to make it work.

Phrases

- "As long as the work gets done, it doesn't matter how many hours you work."
- "I don't care what hours you work, as long as you're putting in your forty hours per week and keeping up the great work you've been doing."
- "I need all team members to be available at the same time."
- "It's essential for you to be available to clients during business hours."
- "Let's stop keeping hours but focus on a simple contract for work provided. We are doing this on a trial basis for now. We need to see how well the system works for the team."
- "We have been working 'off the clock' for three weeks now. It's time to reassess and determine how well it's working, what needs to be altered, and if this seems viable long term."
- "We have varied schedules to accommodate different needs, but everyone here is working hard and getting the job done."

- "What do you need from me in terms of flexible hours?"

- "As long as team members arrange their own schedules for collaboration, meet deadlines, and get the job done, I only need to see you once per week for our videoconference meeting."

- "Our online discussion group allows us to contribute to nonurgent conversations and long-term planning sessions in our own time."

- "I need you to stick to the specified number of log-in hours and client meetings. Beyond that, your schedule is your own as long as you meet team standards."

- "As long as you make up your log-in hours next week, you can take Wednesday off."

- "As long as you produce results, the rest of your time is your own. You can always put in additional time to exceed expectations and increase your earnings, but that's your decision."

- "Not everyone works well with such a flexible schedule, but it's a great asset to those who do. Your teammates are excellent models of self-discipline and are resources for learning how to make the most of this opportunity."

- "We are flexible about our flex-time solutions, so let's find a plan that works well for you."

Chapter 9

Perks, Benefits, and Rewards

"If I could solve all the problems myself, I would."
—Thomas Edison
(explaining why he had a
team of twenty-one assistants)

P erks, benefits, and rewards show appreciation and make team members feel valued. Create a system that rewards both teams and individuals. Share your success with team members and spotlight theirs. A little recognition goes a long way toward building a strong, confident team.

What can you do to spotlight your team? Find opportunities to offer rewards and incentives. A motivated team is a strong team and perks, benefits, and rewards are powerful motivators.

Spotlight Your Team

The Team Mindset

- Support your team members in achieving recognition.
- Always give credit where credit is due.
- Share credit for your own success with your team.
- A positive press release about your team or individual team members is good press for you.
- Don't feel threatened by a team member's success; it reflects well on you, and your support as team leader is motivational.
- Create a regular system for recognition, such as a "Team Member Spotlight" in the company blog or newsletter.
- Encourage team member blogs and media contacts. Establish guidelines, as a team, for representing the team.
- Never accept an award without thanking your team first.
- If your team is small, thank them by name when speaking publicly.
- Show your appreciation and motivate the team by including them in your photo opportunities.
- Look for opportunities to showcase your team's talents.

Phrases

- "First, I'd like to thank my team…"
- "I have nominated the team for an award for innovative thinking."
- "This award is a reflection of my outstanding team and belongs to them as much as it does to me."
- "Congratulations on your latest accomplishment! Who would like to write the press release?"

- "We are pleased to have a new team member joining us today. This is a great opportunity to get out a press release."
- "I think a blog is a great idea. I'd like to see one that gives the whole team a chance to comment, with rotating entries."
- "We'll be taking a team picture for our Web site."
- "I want our clients to know our team. We'll be starting a 'Team Member Spotlight' series."
- "I'm being interviewed tomorrow morning. I'd like everyone in the photo with me."
- "I have been rewarded for this team's efforts and I'd like to share that reward with you."
- "The reward I received is thanks to you. I would like to treat each of you and a guest to a special dinner."
- "I would prefer to have a team member's voice on the podcasts. Who would like to be the first voice of our team?"
- "I'd like the team to collaborate on a team bio page for the Web site. Please include a group photo."
- "We'll have a chance to showcase your talent in the upcoming [technical show, competition, etc.]."
- "I want to see individual bios with photos on the team's bio page. Include a personal statement, if you'd like. Let customers see who we are and what we're about."

Team Perks

The Team Mindset

- What are the perks of being on your team?
- What can you offer to everyone?
- Team members will be proud to show what they have earned by being members of your team.
- Perks are incentives to entice prospective team members.
- Recognition is a perk. Don't underestimate the importance of spotlighting team members or the team as a whole.
- When naming the team as a whole, also name individual members whenever possible.
- Perks are not rewards and should not be held back from any team member. They are typically offered up front and a team leader is only as good as his or her word.

Phrases

- "All members of this team receive special discounts on [software, training, online services, etc.]."
- "All members of this team receive free membership in [VIP clubs, paid areas online, professional associations, etc.]."
- "You all receive special passes as members of this team."
- "Everyone on the team is getting the new product for their hard work on the team."
- "As a member of this team, you are allowed early submission to the journal editor."
- "All team member names are listed in the new 'Who's Who' book."

- "All team members can choose between accepting last year's product as a free gift or a discount on this year's."
- "Because summers are slow here, we have early closings on Fridays in July and August. Of course, if emergencies arise, we have to work through."
- "Everyone on this team gets a monthly discount card to Starbucks."
- "All team members receive employee discounts."

Team-Building Rewards

The Team Mindset

- Team rewards that involve team activities serve not only to reward but to bring the team closer.
- Team rewards might include a retreat, dinner out, or an event.
- Team rewards offered on evenings or weekends should include spouses and significant others.
- When spouses and significant others are included, single people should also be invited to bring someone.
- Never require attendance for any reward that needs to be redeemed during the recipient's personal time.
- Give the same reward to everyone, to be used in each individual's own way. One team reward could be a morning off, taken by team members at staggered times.
- Lunch at a nice restaurant is a team reward that bonds the team in a more social setting without cutting into personal time.
- Individual rewards can be given in a team rotation style.
- Don't reward the team with an event without running the dates by your team first.
- Consider giving team certificates and awards.

Phrases

- "Congratulations! I am going to buy the team tickets to [a game, show, event, etc.] to show my appreciation."
- "I have arranged for a weekend beach retreat to reward the team and help us get some fresh air and fresh ideas. Please let me know by the end of the week if you can attend."

- "Outstanding work! I'm taking everyone out to lunch to celebrate. How's Friday?"
- "As a reward for your insights and creative management of this difficult project, let's start our day at nine o'clock tomorrow instead of eight."
- "Each member will be presented with a team certificate of congratulations."
- "I entered an incentive program online. Let me know which group rewards you, as a team, would prefer."
- "Great work! Let's all go to lunch to celebrate."
- "Everyone is invited to bring a guest to the celebration dinner."
- "Bring your families so they can celebrate with you."
- "Our new online reward system is in place. You'll receive a reward for each new level the team achieves. The whole team will be shopping from the same tier, so pull together to keep bringing it up a notch."
- "You've all put in so much overtime to achieve this goal. Take the next two Fridays off as a reward."
- "Everyone is getting a bonus as a reward. I wish it could be more. Thank you again for your exceptional work."
- "This is an outstanding team and I'm happy to present you with this reward."
- "I have nominated the team for an award, so please attend the awards dinner and feel free to bring a guest."
- "Even though we did not win the award this time, this is a team of winners and I'm honored to be working with you."

Individual Recognition

The Team Mindset

- Strong teams are made up of strong individuals with strong skills. Reward teams, but also reward the individuals who make up the team.
- Individual recognition keeps people from feeling like disposable cogs.
- If one team member does a stand-out job, acknowledge that person publicly.
- Encourage team members to recognize the accomplishments of teammates.
- Organize a celebration for a team member's accomplishment—or see that someone does.
- Use a points system and online award catalog that will track points and offer appropriate awards to teams and/or individuals.
- Don't underestimate the value of a title, but be cautious of how conferring one will affect the status of other team members.
- Find small ways to thank individuals.
- Offer congratulations in writing.
- Avoid favoritism.
- Do not offer a reward to one team member until you know the level of involvement put in by other team members.

Phrases

- "We all worked hard and I thank the whole team. Additionally, I want to recognize Jeff for the extra hours and his outstanding problem-solving skills."

- "Beyond the team reward, I present this special award to Brenda for her role as temporary team leader. Brenda, you did a fantastic job!"
- "Josh was at the forefront of securing our biggest contract this year. I want to offer him a special reward at our team luncheon."
- "Everyone on the team has access to select awards based on our new points system."
- "We now offer individual as well as group rewards."
- "The gift basket is to thank you for the extra work you put in when two team members were suddenly out sick."
- "Special thanks to Val for initiating this project. I offer this reward to the whole team for pulling behind it to make it a success."
- "Congratulations! You're an asset to the team!"
- "We couldn't have pulled this off without the contacts and initiative of two team members, Louise and Karthik. Thank you!"
- "Because of your outstanding work, I'm putting you in charge of the next project."
- "As a reward, I want to send you for management training."
- "I want to invest in your future here and would like to offer you tuition reimbursement."
- "We have two new opportunities opening up. Because of your dedication to the team and your individual accomplishments, I want to offer you first choice."

Incentives

The Team Mindset

- Incentive programs can allow teams or individuals to choose their own prizes.
- Many incentive programs work on a points system, making prizes available through an online catalog.
- Offer incentives for activities that benefit the team.
- Incentives should be offered to everyone.
- Incentive programs can be informal or formal, based on points systems.
- Some actions worthy of reward may not fit into a point system. Some programs based on points systems can be used in conjunction with other formal or informal incentive/reward programs.
- Points systems should be clearly defined, with points equally accessible to all team members.
- Use incentives even for small, daily tasks when the team is getting sluggish.
- Find additional incentive ideas throughout this chapter and more specific incentive program options in the next section: "The Healthy Team."

Phrases

- "The new incentive program offers several tiers of rewards so that every contribution is rewarded, and so is extra effort."
- "Everyone on the team is going to receive the new product. Thanks for making it all happen!"
- "The incentive program is designed not only to reward your hard work but to be mile markers along the way."

➡

- "Everyone has equal access to earn points."
- "I offer three choices of rewards so that everyone receives a fitting reward."
- "I offer three choices of team reward; I'd like the team to select together."
- "If we can all complete this design to the customer's satisfaction by Thursday morning, we can take Thursday afternoon off."
- "If we complete the project by March, I will reward the team with an extra day for play at the summer conference."
- "If we can solve this issue, this team will be assigned some of the more sought-after projects."
- "If we can get through all these calls by noon, lunch is on me."
- "If we meet our quota this month, everyone gets to choose something from tier one of our incentive program."
- "This team has done a lot of extra-heavy work by coming in early and working late. If we can meet this goal, I'll have chair massages set up all next week."
- "If we can beat our record this month, everyone gets a gift certificate for [an electronics store, a nice restaurant, a popular store, etc.]."

The Healthy Team

The Team Mindset

- Only a healthy team can be a strong team.
- Provide wellness incentives.
- Provide what you can for health insurance.
- Provide wellness incentives to the team as a whole, but be aware that the outcome may be unfair to some and try to compensate.
- Promoting team actions and mindsets is important, but wellness is an individual choice and incentives are, for the most part, best offered to individuals.
- A wellness support system is likely to develop even if incentives are given to individuals.
- If the goal is collective, an additional wellness incentive will inspire team spirit.
- Wellness incentives can be small, depending on resources.
- Team weight loss programs can track team weight loss for a fun and inspiring big number. You will, of course, need everyone's consensus on this and must be certain that all participants are fully comfortable with the idea.

Phrases

- "We are offering wellness incentives for everyone who attends one of our new seminars."
- "Pick a buddy or two to attend wellness seminars. You already have a trusted support system. Use it for your health."
- "Congratulations! This team has lost a total of 102 pounds!"

➡

- "When the team's total gym time reaches 100 hours, we'll celebrate with an early closing."
- "The smoke-free program is available to all team members. I urge you to take advantage of this highly effective free program."
- "Our nutrition seminars will earn 4 points per session toward your individual [or team] total."
- As a reward for achieving your team points goal, we're going to close early on Friday for a company picnic. I hope you and your families can attend for fresh air, fun, and good, healthy food."
- "For anyone who chooses to take part in the wellness walk, we have a wellness walk package, which includes a tee-shirt, water bottle, and gift certificate to the juice bar down the street."
- "Everyone who takes part in two wellness walks will receive a new iPod."
- "I would prefer healthy team members to workaholics. If team members have to sacrifice health and a home life, then we're doing something wrong."
- "Please read your insurance policies so that you won't lose benefits by not following necessary procedures."
- "The health of team members is good for the health of the team."

Part Three

Team-Building Exercises

What do you know about team-building exercises? Are you aware of your options? Have you considered hiring a professional? If you have, do you know what questions to ask? Team-building exercises can have a positive impact; however, exercises that have no positive impact and waste time will frustrate the team and cause them to lose confidence in you and the process. Know all you can about your options so that your team gets the maximum benefit from team-building efforts.

Chapter 10

Team-Building Exercises

"Individual commitment to a group effort—that is what makes a team work, a company work, a society work, a civilization work."

—Vince Lombardi

One way that team members show their commitment is by participating, wholeheartedly, in team exercises. Teams that want to learn and grow take every opportunity. They do, however, need to have the benefits clearly explained. If doing so before an exercise would take steam out of the exercise itself, assure team members that the exercise will be useful. After building trust and conducting useful exercises, the team will take for granted that, more often than not, exercises will be useful. Dedicated teams don't want their time wasted when they could be working toward the team's ultimate goals.

Team techniques can be as simple as using icebreaker questions, some of which you will find later in this chapter. Let the team get to know one another on a personal level, but teach them to navigate the boundaries of "too personal."

As relationships within the team develop into friendships, boundaries will change for those individuals; but beyond that, within the team, overly personal questions unnecessarily create a feeling of privacy invasion.

Team-Building Professionals

The Team Mindset

- You can do a lot to build and strengthen your team, but you may want to consider hiring a team-building professional.

- Shop around before you make an investment.

- Consultants and team builders use several different methods; consider your needs.

- Ask questions regarding methods and transfer of learned skills to your team's work environment.

- Some team builders work with teams on practical, immediately applicable team skills.

- Some team builders and consultants use the aid of psychological profiles. These may be especially useful if your team has difficult interpersonal issues.

- Don't discount team-building exercises or programs if they do not seem immediately applicable. Instead, ask the team builder how he or she intends to help your team transfer and integrate learned skills.

- Different team builders and team consultants offer different levels of customization. Again, decide what is important to you—and shop carefully.

- Have the professional advise you about what to expect and how to follow-up. The person or team you hire should also have follow-up as part of the program.

- Ask for references.

➡

Phrases

(Questions to Ask Team Builders)

- "Are you insured for this type of off-site exercise?"
- "What is your process?"
- "What would you need from me or my team in advance of training?"
- "Do you have references whom I can contact?"
- "How do you measure success?"
- "I have two team members who have trouble getting along. What special attention can you give to that situation?"
- "What team-building skills do you focus on?"
- "How do you determine which skills to focus on?"
- "What is my role in the process?"
- "Do you use psychological profiling?"
- "I have particular cross-cultural issues. How do you handle that?"
- "How do you use the information from psychological profiles?"
- "What does your follow-up process involve?"
- "Do you have on- and off-site options?"
- "What results can you share with me from teams you've worked with in the past?"

Types of Team-Building Exercises

The Team Mindset

- Team-building exercises can be conducted either on-site or off-site.

- You, as team leader, can run team-building exercises or you may choose to hire a professional team builder.

- Scenario-based exercises allow your team to problem-solve through complex situations without leaving the meeting room.

- Adventure-style team building is best left to trained, insured professionals.

- Take advantage of opportunities to have your team brainstorm or problem-solve.

- Brainstorming, and problem-solving sessions are part of many team-building processes.

- Team building goes beyond formal exercises to regular activities worked on by the team.

- Let your team members develop their own team-building exercises.

- Create team-building exercises on your own or delve into the wealth of do-it-yourself team-building exercises available in books and online.

- Any method or activity that motivates, educates, inspires, or brings team members together is part of team building.

- Role playing is an interesting team exercise. Everyone should be involved in some way. Have those who are not taking part in the role play participate in feedback and commentary afterwards.

- Integrating team-building exercises into your schedule will help the team continually strengthen its communication and team skills.
- Some highly effective team-building exercises cost little or nothing, and many are small time investments, as well.

Phrases

- "I would like each of you to devise a team-building exercise."
- "You will work, as teams, to devise the next team-building exercises."
- "Work, as a team, to solve this issue."
- "I have hired a team-building expert to keep us energized and working optimally as a team."
- "I have e-mailed a link to our new team-building company's Web site so everyone can see who it is we are working with and take a look at their style and philosophy."
- "I have an exciting series of team-building exercises planned. I know this team will excel."
- "Team-building exercises will help us keep learning about ourselves and one another and how we can best function as a team."
- "I realize that you might not immediately see the purpose behind some of our team-building exercises, but please hang in and participate fully. It will all become clear later, and I think you will find the results interesting."

➡

- "Please take your role in this scenario seriously. It's an exercise that will translate to critical skills of team functioning."

- "You have all been very agreeable and positive about our new promotional plan. I would like everyone, just as an exercise, to come up with three flaws or possible drawbacks. Then, work as a team to decide what, if anything, should be refined to strengthen the plan."

- "I want everyone to break into teams and take an assigned role in the discussion: optimist or pessimist. Then, switch sides. We'll share insights and responses afterward." [Often, a whole-hearted optimist will find a chink that could be repaired, and a pessimist will learn from finding a positive angle.]

- "I have devised these exercises with this team in mind."

- "The team-building professional will be here to interview us. Please be forthright and honest. Only by presenting ourselves honestly, problems and all, will we take full advantage of this program."

What's Right for Your Team?

The Team Mindset

- Know your team; find out what they need.

- What kind of team building is right for your team? Not every method is right for every team.

- Remind team members that change is a process.

- Team-building exercises make a strong team stronger.

- If your team is under heavy time pressures, use team-building exercises that can be applied to the work that needs to be done.

- If your team's problems stem from a battle of two wills, have someone work solely with those two people, at least as a start.

- Use personality profiles only with the help of an expert. It is not your role to psychoanalyze, and could complicate your role with the team.

- Would a change of scenery be a strong advantage?

- Do you have a lot of sports-oriented team members? If so, consider starting a sports team. Remember that to build team spirit, a sports team would have to be appropriate for and inclusive of everyone.

Phrases

- "What would you hope to gain from this exercise?"

- "List two things you hope will change as a result of a team-building excursion."

- "Realize that changes don't happen overnight."

- "Does anyone on the team have a recommendation for a team-building company?"

➡

- "Has anyone on the team tried a particular team-building exercise that was especially helpful?"

- "What team-building experiences have you had that were not helpful and left you feeling you had wasted your time? Please answer without naming names. We just want to learn from those experiences."

- "I realize that this team is still forming and you're all still refining your roles. This is a difficult stage, but I have no doubt that we'll come through this phase as a strong, supportive team. I think a team-building excursion might help bring us closer to acting as a team."

- "I'm going to start working team-building exercises into our meetings. Exercises will be brief, but effective."

- "Yes, we saw some positive change after our team-building exercises. Don't be discouraged by having some difficulties again. Change is a process."

- "I am having a team-building expert meet with us to determine exactly what kind of team-building process would be most beneficial to us."

- "Please submit your concerns about the team and areas you would like to target with our team-building efforts."

- "Do you feel there is trust among team members?"

- "Would you say that team members are clear about their roles and comfortable with them?"

- "Is there resentment or competition within the team?"

- "I would like everyone to read books and listen to CDs from my library. Once per week, we will share what we've learned with each other."

Team-Building Follow-Through

The Team Mindset

- Follow-through is essential for any team-building exercise.

- After an exercise is completed, elicit opinions from team members. In many cases, it is beneficial to survey team members again after one month.

- If you work with a team-building professional, build follow-up into the process.

- Follow-up is motivational to the team because it lets them know that no time or energy has been wasted. Benefits of the process are weighed before being repeated in the same style.

- Determine, prior to giving exercises, what success would look like. Evaluate in terms of measurable results.

- Be aware of subtle results that are beyond objective, measurable ones. Especially where interpersonal issues are involved, even subtle shifts can have a powerful impact on the team.

- A number of avenues for follow-up are available. Use the most appropriate ones, whether verbally or in writing, individually or as a team.

Phrases

- "What worked well?"
- "What didn't work well?"
- "What changes have you seen in the team since the last team-building exercise?"
- "What did you learn?"
- "What changes would you have made to the process?"

➡

- "Did you believe in the process going in?"
- "Would you recommend this process to other teams?"
- "Is this a process you feel would be helpful for this team to repeat?"
- "What did you think about the exercise leader?"
- "How would you assess the way the exercise was conducted?"
- "What did you learn about yourself in the process?"
- "What did you learn about the team?"
- "What outcome would you have liked that you didn't see?"
- "What surprised you?"
- "Would you use this [team-building company, process, exercise, format, etc.] again?"

Icebreaker Questions

The Team Mindset

- Icebreaker questions are a very simplified team-bonding exercise.

- Use icebreakers at the start of an initiative, when team members are meeting one another, and, once in a while, to open meetings. Doing so will allow team members to learn a little more about one another.

- Even though icebreakers can lighten the mood, don't try to force the issue or continue to use them if your team is not enjoying them.

- Don't try to fit icebreakers in when you don't have time. Doing so will only backfire and add to tensions.

- Depending on how many questions you have in store, give one question to the whole team or let them pick questions from a hat.

- Break the group into twos or threes or go around the whole group and let people answer. Allow people to say, "Can you come back to me?" or "I'd rather not say." It should all be friendly and laid back.

- Be extremely careful not to ask questions that are too personal.

- Steer clear of politics, religion, and tragedy. Remember your goal in using the icebreaker is to create a friendly team atmosphere. Focus on questions that bring people together; don't risk using questions that could easily put people at odds.

➡

- Ensure the team that icebreakers are intended to be fun and meant to be light. If any question touches on an area they don't want to answer, that's fine. It's just a friendly icebreaker.

Icebreaker Questions

- "What was the best year of your life? Why?"
- "What brought you into this field?"
- "What was your best childhood memory?"
- "What questions are you most tired of being asked?"
- "What question do you wish you'd be asked more?"
- "What is your all-time favorite movie?"
- "What's the worst movie you ever saw?"
- "What was the best book you ever read?"
- "What was the most inspirational book you ever read?"
- "What was the most inspirational recent moment you can recall?"
- "What inspires you?"
- "What is your favorite art form?"
- "What song do you know all the lyrics to?" [If not, "What song do you wish you did?"]
- "If you could go anywhere for the weekend, where would it be?"
- "If you could be any superhero, which one would you be and why?"
- "Who is the most inspirational person you know?"

Resource File

I f you choose to find team-building exercises on your own (to use in addition to or instead of hiring a professional), many team-building professionals share simple exercises in team-building books and online. Search online for team-building professionals and/or do-it-yourself team-building exercises.

Exercise Books

Following are a few useful books that offer team-building exercises you can try with your team:

The Big Book of Team Building Games: Trust-Building Activities, Team Spirit, Exercises, and Fun Things to Do, John W. Newstrom and Edward E. Scannell (New York: McGraw-Hill, 1998).

Indoor/Outdoor Team Building Games for Trainers: Powerful Activities from the World of Adventure-Based Team Building and Ropes Courses, Harrison Snow (New York: McGraw-Hill, 1997).

The Practical Executive: Team Building, Eric Skopec and Dayle M. Smith (New York: McGraw-Hill, 1997).

Teambuilding that Gets Results: Essential Plans and Activities for Creating Effective Teams, Linda Eve Diamond and Harriet Diamond (Naperville, IL: Sourcebooks, Inc., 2007).

The Team Building Workbook, Gib Akin (New York: McGraw-Hill, 2001).

Online Searches

If you search online for additional resources, remember that "teambuilding" and "team building" may bring up some different results. Most people will enter both into key word lists, but not everyone does. As most compound words find their ways slowly into the language, when team building was new as a concept, it was only expressed as two separate words. It has been a concept in use for a long time, but language is slow to catch up. In this time of slow linguistic transition, it is acceptable to use as one or two words, which is helpful to realize when searching online.

Conclusion

I n the daily barrage of activity and to-do's, remember the importance of building and nourishing your team. Work in team-building exercises, refine and add team processes, and guide your team through the stages of development to ultimate team success. Find additional resources and encourage your team to do the same.

Team building is an art and a skill. Sculpting your team requires your talent and skills and the proper tools. Team leader tools include the team mindset and phrases that make your team feel respected and appreciated. Your words are the most powerful team-building tool you have. Keep them positive and encouraging, and use them wisely.

Accept responsibility and share praise and remember that you, too, are part of the team, pitching in when necessary. Build trust with your team. Be the team leader they can count on, the leader who tells the truth and shares the glory. Your team needs you to be fully integrated in a collaborative mindset. You have what it takes to build a strong team. Use the phrases in this book and find perfect phrases of your own. A strong team begins with you.

About the Author

Linda **Eve Diamond** is the coauthor of *Perfect Phrases for Motivating and Rewarding Employees; Team Building that Gets Results; Executive Writing, American Style;* and the author of *Rule #1: Stop Talking; A Guide to Listening.* Her expertise comes from over a decade in the corporate training field, writing, designing, and delivering customized training programs in all areas of communication for a broad spectrum of clients.

Linda's writing and design of print materials earned her an award from the New Jersey Association for Lifelong Learning, and her poetry won a small press award. Her poems are now available as a collection titled: *The Human Experience.* Currently a full-time freelance writer and author, she serves on the executive board of the International Listening Association (ILA) and as editor of *The Listening Post,* an ILA newsletter publication.

Linda has two Web sites, each featuring a blog that welcomes your comments. Visit her sites at www.LindaEveDiamond.com and www.ListenersUnite.com.

PERFECT PHRASES
for...

MANAGERS

Perfect Phrases for
Managers and Supervisors

Perfect Phrases for Setting
Performance Goals

Perfect Phrases for
Performance Reviews

Perfect Phrases for
Motivating and Rewarding
Employees

Perfect Phrases for
Documenting Employee
Performance Problems

Perfect Phrases for Business
Proposals and Business Plans

Perfect Phrases for
Customer Service

Perfect Phrases for
Executive Presentations

Perfect Phrases for Business
Letters

Perfect Phrases for the
Sales Call

Perfect Phrases for Perfect
Hiring

Perfect Phrases for Building
Strong Teams

Perfect Phrases for Dealing
with Difficult People

YOUR CAREER

Perfect Phrases for the
Perfect Interview

Perfect Phrases for
Resumes

Perfect Phrases for Negotiating
Salary & Job Offers

Perfect Phrases for Cover
Letters

Learn more.  Do more.

Visit mhprofessional.com/perfectphrases for a complete product listing.